WOMAN AWAKE

By Christina Feldman

*Silence: How to Find Inner Peace in a Busy World* (2003)

*Woman Awake: Women Practicing Buddhism* (2005)

# Woman Awake

*Women Practicing Buddhism*

Christina Feldman

Shambhala
Boulder, 2005

Shambhala Publications, Inc.
4720 Walnut Street
Boulder, Colorado 80301
www.shambhala.com

A Rodmell Press book

Cover images: "Anne with Plant" (detail) copyright © 1990–1991 by Brett Bigbee/Alexandre Gallery, New York; "Buddha Hand" copyright © Luca I. Tetoni/Corbis; author photograph by Libby Vigeon.

First edition (1990) published by Arkana/Penguin (UK).

9 8 7 6 5 4

Printed in the United States of America

⊛ This edition is printed on acid-free paper that meets the American National Standards Institute Z39.48 Standard.
♻ Shambhala Publications makes every effort to print on recycled paper. For more information please visit www.shambhala.com.
Shambhala Publications is distributed worldwide by Penguin Random House, Inc., and its subsidiaries.

Editor: Linda Cogozzo                     Cover and Book Designer: Gopa & Ted2, Inc.
Proofreader: Katherine L. Kaiser          Lithographer: Phoenix Color Corp.
Indexer: Ty Koontz
Text set in Dante and Cochin

*Library of Congress Cataloging-in-Publication Data*

Feldman, Christina.
Woman awake: women practicing Buddhism/Christina Feldman.—2nd ed.
p. cm.
Includes index.
ISBN 978-1-930485-06-8 (pbk.: alk. paper)
1. Buddhist women—Religious life. 2. Meditation—Buddhism. I. Title.
BQ5450.F45 2005
294.3'4435'082—dc22
2004023488

# ⦂ *Contents*

# Acknowledgments

THIS BOOK has been inspired by so many rich sources. It contains the teachings and the voices of the numerous teachers who have had a profound influence on my own understanding and vision.

I feel deep gratitude for the presence and teaching of the teachers in my own practice who offered their wisdom, patience, and compassion so freely. The greatest gift they offered was the vision they treasured of freedom and love.

I thank my parents for giving me the freedom to follow my own path and direction. My husband and children continue to give support and encouragement.

I would like to acknowledge the encouragement and support of so many women I have had the privilege of being with in retreats. This book is their story: without their honesty and courage, there would be no story to tell. I feel deeply grateful for their presence, and continue to be awed by their quest for a way of being in the world and with themselves that is rooted in integrity and wisdom.

I thank Roz for her encouragement and patience in helping me to begin this venture. I deeply thank Shannon Gilligan for her unflagging enthusiasm and skill. Without her heartfelt dedication, I would still be muddling my way through the introduction.

# Introduction

A WOMAN EMBARKING on a spiritual journey travels a path on which there are few sure guides to inspire and affirm her. The institutions and traditions we are heirs to have been primarily formulated, structured, and maintained by men, with their own vision and application of spirituality. Each of these authorities offers a sanctioned pathway to living and being. Each pathway has its own expectations, values, and models to strive for. There is an underlying message common to all of these voices—to conform is to be offered safety, acceptance, and, most of all, love. To step outside of these institutions is to lose approval and shelter, and to be alone.

This situation is exacerbated by the fact that we carry with us a history of learning to listen outwardly rather than inwardly. As children we have thrust upon us the values of others telling us how we should be, what a nice and good person is. We respond to these demands in order to win a degree of affirmation, approval, and safety in our lives, and the pattern becomes set. Through fear and inner alienation, we form static relationships to authority. It is perceived as all-powerful and also infallible.

Not surprisingly, when we begin on a spiritual path we find ourselves looking outwardly to tradition and authority, for they appear to hold the answers we are seeking. Thus we acquire approval and safety in the conformity that these spiritual authorities require, only to discover that approval and safety are poor substitutes for freedom. There is no tradition or person who is qualified to tell us who we should be, what we must strive for or achieve. Established religions have repeatedly armored themselves against women, seeking to silence their voices. Our blind acceptance of models and expectations, and the inner denial and division they represent, can only serve to suffocate the inner spiritual vision from which our freedom is born.

We need to be willing to risk the loss of external affirmation and approval if we are to know ourselves deeply. We need to be willing to risk listening to ourselves as well as others. The validity of our spiritual path can only be qualified by our own experience and understanding. Through a path of contemplation and meditation, we can untangle the conditioning that leads us to prostrate ourselves before authority. By cultivating a deep inner aloneness, we can nurture our inner resources of awareness and understanding. A vision of our uniqueness is born, an authentic vision of who we are, as opposed to who we have been told we should be.

We discover a freedom not limited by models, or dichotomies, by divisions between inner and outer, mind and body, spiritual and worldly. Instead, a vision—and a path of spirituality—arises that affirms and celebrates the interconnectedness of all life. This is not to reject outright and with hostility religion and tradition. Tradition is rich in experience and has the power to inspire us and guide us. But we need to be vigilant in our listening, so as not to repeat the errors of the past. We must find the balance between, on the one hand, being able to listen outwardly and not to be overwhelmed by what we hear and, on the other, the ability to learn without feeling compelled to conform. With sensitivity we can listen to and learn from the richness of tradition, while still cherishing, preserving, and nurturing the integrity of listening within ourselves.

For me, spirituality is awakening. This awakened seeing embraces a vision of oneness, truth, and reality that transcends difference, division, and separation. Spiritual vision is a mystical one—cut free of linear space or time—which frees us to extend ourselves with love to every area of our lives. A spiritual life is a celebration of inner wholeness, joy, connectedness, and serenity. The love that is born of this vision of oneness impels us to act and to direct our lives with sensitivity and integrity. The spiritual woman is a woman of joy, who knows what it means to trust in herself. She lives her spirituality and, free from fear, she rejoices in her own uniqueness.

# Introduction to the Second Edition

IN 1984, the Insight Meditation Society, in Barre, Massachusetts, sponsored a rare initiative: the first women's retreat in the Theravadan Buddhist tradition. It was soon followed by a similar retreat at Spirit Rock, in Woodacre, California. It was a significant beginning, with fifty women gathering together to contemplate what it means to walk a spiritual path as a woman, in a woman's body, and with a woman's story and voice.

The first years were tentative but rich, as we discovered together that we had much to explore and understand. Times of silent meditation were interspersed with focused dialogues exploring questions of power, authority, autonomy, and what it means to be truly awake in every area of our lives. Twenty years later, this retreat continues annually, and convenes a community of women who are awakening and deepening in understanding together. We have become more silent, more contemplative, over the years. Within the retreats there is a palpable dignity, trust and respect, and a sense of community. These two decades have borne witness to countless social and political changes in our world that embody the maturing wisdom of women. Underlying these outer changes is a powerful dedication and understanding: the commitment not only to liberation in the world, but to a profound inner liberation.

Like all spiritual traditions, the women's retreats have a history. When I first began to practice meditation in India in the early 1970s, I embraced the teachings and path of Buddhism as a homecoming. For several years, I lived a dedicated meditative life, blithely assuming that gender was not an issue. It came as something of a shock when I first undertook to practice in a monastic setting to have it brought forcibly home to me that my assumptions were wrong. Although women practitioners were frequently and effusively praised for the sincerity and depth of their practice, it was also true that the monastic forms would have struggled to survive without the devoted support, commitment, and work of the lay and ordained women.

Equally, it was apparent that gender was a very real but mostly unspoken issue. Women were barred from full ordination, and consequently barred from holding authority within the tradition. There was a dearth of women teachers, and the most senior woman practitioner in the monastery was required to bow before the most junior monk; in age-old tradition, the women were required to attend to the domestic duties that benefited all, sat at the end of the food table, and were allocated the worst accommodations. My heart broke when an elderly nun told me she served and meditated to accumulate sufficient merit to be reborn a man, because then she would be worthy of enlightenment. My profound gratitude for the monastic lineage that had kept alive the teaching of liberation co-existed with a growing sense of unease that it was this same lineage that carried an institutionalized rejection of women.

When I raised questions about the obvious injustices and diminishment of women that were part of the fabric of monastic life, I was assured repeatedly and at times heatedly, that it was just form and that a good meditator would utilize the forms to deepen her capacity to surrender and achieve selflessness. The crunch came for me one evening when I was invited to give a discourse, only to discover that it would be unacceptable for me to occupy the traditional seat given to the evening speaker because it would place me, a woman, physically higher than the monks. Ingenious alternatives were offered: I could sit in the abbot's hut and speak through the public address system; I could sit at the back of the hall; or someone else could deliver the talk if I wrote it out. Meetings were held to try to work out an acceptable alternative. In the end, it was grudgingly agreed that I would take the traditional seat; many of the monks decided they had more pressing engagements that evening.

When I began to lead meditation retreats in the West, it became apparent that I and countless other women carried within our psyches and hearts the imprints of centuries of spiritual, religious traditions in which women had little voice or stature. The wealth of literature written by and about liberated women was noticeably absent or ignored. There existed volumes of literature that described the dangers and distractions posed by women to those who sought liberation. It was rare to find a woman teacher, and the statues and icons occupying the altars were rarely, if ever, female. Form, I came to understand, was not irrelevant. The forms and structures of our lives communicate what we value, treasure, and aspire to. Visible or invisible, they express what we are dedicated and committed to: they are our language of being in the world.

Walt Whitman writes that everything we have done, do, and will do is done in our bodies. Equally, everything we have done, do, and will do is done in our minds, hearts, and lives. If we, as women, are to awaken, to realize the depths of compassion and wisdom possible for us, it too will be realized in our bodies, minds, and hearts. We do not begin on a spiritual path divorced from our sexuality, histories, or lives: all of this we bring with us. If there is any singular characteristic that distinguishes a woman's spirituality, it is the unwavering understanding that deep realisation does not demand transcendence of this life and all it holds and of which we are part. We learn to turn toward our bodies, minds, and hearts, understanding that within them we discover a microcosmic view of all bodies, minds, and hearts. We learn to embrace the reality of our lives as the classroom in which wisdom and compassion are understood. Awakened women are embodied women: women who have renounced the dualism of heaven and earth, spiritual and mundane, transcendent and worldly. Forsaking these dualities, a spiritual path is a path not only of liberation but one dedicated to healing all schisms. It is a path of profound dignity, respect, and freedom.

Throughout history, women embarking on a spiritual path have been courageous women. Their dedication to liberation and dignity has often been a lonely journey with little external support or encouragement. Cultural and spiritual models and expectations have encouraged women to make their home in invisibility and in the shadows of life. Historically, compliance has been rewarded with approval and affirmation, but rarely with respect or dignity. To liberate ourselves from the roles, models, and invisibility that have been our legacy is a journey not only of outer change but of genuine inner transformation. We have needed to learn to listen inwardly rather than to the powerful voices of outer authority and expectation. We have needed to find the willingness to risk the loss of affirmation and praise. Every spiritual journey asks us to cultivate a deep, inner aloneness as the first step in reclaiming inner wholeness. Authentic spiritual journeys teach us to marry this inner solitude to an unwavering dedication to exploring our undeniable connectedness with all life. Our path, we have come to understand, is not only a commitment to inner awakening but a commitment to the awakening of life. It is a path not only of insight, but also of loving kindness and compassion.

Tradition is rich in wisdom and experience, and has the power to teach and inspire us. The wisdom of women is a tradition that teaches us to listen inwardly and know that genuine liberation lies in our own hearts and our own understanding. Spiritual vision is a mystical one that is free of linear space or time. It is also an embodied vision that frees us to extend ourselves with love to every dimension of our lives. A spiritual life is a celebration of inner wholeness, joy, connectedness, and serenity. A woman on a spiritual path is a woman of joy, who knows what it means to trust in herself. She lives her wisdom and, free from fear, rejoices in her own uniqueness.

# Chapter 1
## *Beginnings*

Our lives are marked by the new beginnings we are repeatedly called upon to make. The life stages we inevitably experience, the crises that challenge us, and the metamorphoses we go through inwardly are all turning points that impel us to make new beginnings. The changes we encounter in our lives and our unfolding inner changes demand that we learn to respond to new situations, and call upon us to find radically new ways of responding. With each new step we take in our lives, with each stage we pass through, we leave behind us the familiarity of the past and the ways of responding that were appropriate to the past. We enter untraveled territory that demands a renewal of our consciousness.

Some of the beginnings we are called upon to make are integral life phases that we share. The onset of menstruation, leaving our childhood homes, establishing of identities and life directions for ourselves, and menopause and old age are all life phases that mark new beginnings for us. We cannot control these phases in our lives, and we cannot avoid them. Each challenges us to question our identities and the meanings of our lives.

There are other parallels in women's experience that equally mark the making of new beginnings. We pursue and change careers. We choose to marry or to bear children, all changes which call for new ways of responding and changes in our identities. We may choose to be alone or we may choose to form an intimate relationship with another. We may choose to rebel against sanctioned ways of being or to follow in the footsteps of our foremothers. With each choice and change we make, we experience the dying of an "I" identity and the birth of a new way of being and seeing.

Some of the beginnings we make are forced and imposed upon us by life changes we cannot control or predict. Loss, death, and separation have the power to hurl us into making beginnings we neither welcome nor feel we can cope with. A loved partner can unexpectedly die; a woman who has relied upon her marriage for identity and meaning is abandoned by her husband, and she is thrust into a vacuum where there is little in the way of certainty to rely upon. She cannot hold on to the past and the future is an abyss of uncertainty, but she knows that if she is to survive she must begin again.

When a woman who has dedicated her life to mothering her children faces their inevitable departure, she is forced to explore the depths of her being so as to find new ways of responding to the identity change thrust upon her or else sink into an endless and destructive grieving. When a woman who has spent her life preserving her youth and attractiveness is forced to confront the specter of ageing, the lines on her face, and the sagging of her body, she is impelled consciously to confront the changes she is undergoing or else to become a parody of the person she used to be.

The changes integral to moving through life challenge us to discover new ways of being, new ways of relating, and a new sense of who we are. Each phase we go through, each change we experience, challenges us to ask that critical and fundamental question, *Who am I?* We are thrown back upon ourselves to question our identities and our relationship to the whole of our lives. Each change and phase overthrows our assumptions and conclusions about ourselves and the meaning of our lives. We can take nothing for granted—neither the security of our personal worlds, nor the familiarity of our identities. We face some of life's fundamental truths—nothing is truly predictable; neither can we control the world we experience nor even the way in which we experience it.

There are times when our beginnings are not forced upon us by life stages or by other change, but thrust upon us by inner discontent and desperation. Times when the direction of life ceases to hold any meaning for us and becomes a prison that suffocates us; times when our identities become a sham, empty of joy or authenticity. A woman who spends the bulk of her adult years in a religious community only to find that she is becoming disillusioned both with the direction of the community and her role within it enters into a crisis where she knows she must make changes, inwardly and outwardly, or live a life of untruth. She knows she must go forward, make a new beginning, or endure a living death of the spirit. Inwardly she knows there is no choice but to begin anew: the very inner tension she experiences dislodges her from the familiarity of her life and identity.

The woman who has lived for years within the confines of a stifling relationship experiences an escalation of tension and discontent that spurs her
to escape. She knows that whatever price she must pay, whatever sacrifice
she must make, she can no longer accept the self-negation she has been living with. She does not know what awaits her—the future is empty of guarantees—but she knows there is no choice but to make a new beginning.

Beginnings are also born of an intuition of unfulfilled inner potential.
Our outer lives, our jobs, and our relationships may be calm and ordered.
Within our own consciousness, there may be no outstanding conflict or discontent. In the midst of that calm, an inner curiosity may lead us to question our identities and the meaning of our lives. We may see the roles,
successes, and achievements we have gained and still find ourselves asking,
*Is this all that I am?* We may sense resources and strengths that lie dormant
within us, possibilities of fulfillment that we have not yet explored. Beginnings are not always born of suffering and conflict. They are equally initiated
by a divine curiosity. It is a curiosity that inspires us creatively to explore the
depths of our own consciousness and being.

The beginnings we make, whether inspired by suffering or by creativity,
will signal upheaval. At times, something or someone will be left behind as
we leave behind a past that has become empty of meaning for us. Our beginnings may well cause change and pain to the structures and people we have
previously relied upon. Questioning our own identities and meanings
inspires us to initiate change. It also forces the people and structures around
us to question their own identities and meanings.

Shelley had spent many years in a contemplative community of nuns.
Over a period of time, she experienced a growing sense of discontent. Serenity became an experience of the past, replaced by feelings of doubt in the
symbols of her life and the church and feelings of rebellion against the teachings she had previously been obedient to. She felt suppressed and stifled,
bereft of vocation. She confided her inner conflict to the sisters in the community and in doing so set off tidal waves of doubt in them. The questioning she initiated escalated to the degree that the very order of the
community was threatened. The guiding nun was called to speak with her
and asked her if she could set aside her doubts and rebellions, if not for her
own sake, for the sake of the community. In facing the choice she was
offered, between suppression and the search for new meanings, she realized

there really was no choice to make. She could not live with what had become empty to her and left the community to explore new meanings and directions in the church.

In making new beginnings, we realize that they may well entail coping with the disapproval and anguish of others. The beginnings we make may be made in the face of doubt and discouragement from people and structures we have previously relied upon for support and encouragement. We must also cope with our own doubt and insecurity as we cut the umbilical cords that have previously sustained us. We are forced to trust in the present and in the unknown, because in our insecurity we may not even have any inner trust to sustain us. We surrender to the only knowing that we have, the knowing that the beginnings we make are essential to knowing who we are.

The beginnings that are rooted in questioning the meanings of our lives are qualitatively different from changes rooted only in a superficial dissatisfaction. Such dissatisfactions lead only to minor modification in our outer lives. Deep questioning makes us willing to undergo radical change and to break with or transform the past. Our beginnings are not always born of a conscious search for an authentic identity or spiritual fulfillment. We do not always have conscious goals we are focused upon or conscious paths that we cultivate. Often, the only thing we are conscious of is an inner stirring that inspires us to explore and open ourselves to the unknown.

The stirrings within me led me, at seventeen, to leave home and travel to India. My journey was not so much a pilgrimage as an escape. It was an easy step to take, simply because I had little to leave behind in the form of clear life direction or involvement. Perhaps I was not an unusual product of the 1960s, filled with confusion and doubt, knowing what I didn't want yet not knowing what I did. I knew what I wanted to leave behind, but had no idea of where I was going. How easy it was to discard with contempt so many of the values, social structures, and goals of my world, yet how difficult to fill the vacuum that remained. I possessed so many ideals of love, peace, and liberation. It was painful to see how radically divorced they were from the actuality of my inner experience.

I had so much apparent freedom: the freedom to forsake a social heritage that no longer felt meaningful, the freedom to say no, and the freedom to make choices. Yet, lacking the understanding to make my choices wisely, I found the options before me merely confusing. My confusion and lack of inner direction were an obvious expression of a lack of inner freedom. Leaving behind so many of the props, values, and expectations I was so eager to condemn served to make me aware of how shackled I was by my own conditioning and its limitations. My mind, my responses, and my past were my constant companions, but without the reinforcement of my props it was much more difficult to distract myself from them or to blame them on anyone or anything else.

Arriving in India did not dispel my confusion but only my illusions. Instead of finding a land resonating with the peace and enlightenment of my images, I found a culture filled with people either battling to survive or, if that battle had been won, people struggling to adopt the values and goals I had wanted to leave behind. Instead of finding the holy men of my expectations residing on every street corner (and at this time in my life I thought of holiness only in the male gender), I encountered men who seemed primarily intent on making contact with whatever part of my anatomy happened to be visible. After three weeks spent distraught and shocked, hiding in a hotel room and venturing out only when protected from head to foot by every item of clothing I possessed, the most pressing urge within me was to escape from India and this life of *purdah*.

It was a revelation to arrive in a small Tibetan village in the foothills of the Himalayas, the home of the Dalai Lama and the spiritual center of Tibetan Buddhism. There was poverty, but tranquility amidst it, and there was deprivation, but a radiance shining in the people enduring it. The gentleness, openness, and love of the Tibetan people deeply touched a chord of response within me. I felt intuitively and immediately that there was a vast amount for me to learn from these people.

It was here that my formal spiritual training began. I listened to the heart of the Buddha's teaching: There is suffering, there is a cause of suffering, there is a total end to suffering, and there is a path to its end. Such a simple teaching: yet for me, one with so much power. A teaching which rendered questionable my view of myself as a powerless victim of circumstances, which gave me a relationship to my life and myself instead of making me a passive spectator of it. Messages of compassion, of oneness, and of joy, which had not been a part of my inner vocabulary, gave meaning to being, to living, and offered a vision of transformation and freedom, inwardly and outwardly.

Over the next few years, I was painfully confronted with the actuality that it was not sufficient merely to treasure a vision of transformation, but it was also necessary consciously to cultivate the path toward it. How easy it was, meditating on my idyllic mountaintop and surrounded by loving people, to believe I was achieving my goal of being free from resentment, hostility, and separation and replacing those feelings with boundless loving kindness and compassion. How quickly were my fragile spiritual images of myself shattered when I descended from my mountain paradise to be enraged with the first bus conductor who seemed compulsively enamored of my body.

How complacently I abided in my spiritual snobbishness, feeling myself to be the owner of the "only" way and so much spiritual knowledge. How painful it was to discover that I still had difficulty in being alone with myself. It became clear that there was something obviously amiss either with my understanding of loving kindness, freedom, and compassion or with my application of those concepts.

It was a necessary disillusionment, the discovery that concepts, beliefs, and ideals do not in themselves possess the power to bring about inner change. Discovering that learning is very different from transformation inspired me to explore the depths of solitude, meditation, and inquiry. I began to spend more time in intensive meditation, being with myself and exploring the dynamics of my own being. It was not always easy. Meeting myself meant the surfacing of past, unresolved conflicts. It meant experiencing the pain of my alienation from myself, confronting the depths of my conditioning, and questioning my own identity and direction. But it was a time of joy and beauty, too, as I learned to listen inwardly, discovered resources I didn't know I had, and began to trust in those resources. It was a time of wonder and revelation as I began to sense intimations of what it meant to be awake and nurture the inner seeds of understanding.

Leaving India was a new beginning that confronted me with the fact that there is no such thing as spiritual retirement and no place for complacency. Spending time in Theravadan Buddhist countries began to stir the awakening of the feminine within myself as I encountered spiritual biases that decreed that my femininity made my spiritual growth less worthy. I began to question my spiritual identity and in that questioning began to realize that it was still to some degree an adopted identity. More exploration and understanding were still called for if I was to develop a spiritual path and identity that fully addressed my own past, my own present, and my own experience.

I was and am deeply grateful to the teachers and traditions that so freely offered the richness of their experience and understanding to me. But I also realized that it was necessary to explore my own uniqueness and experience and to discover my own freedom amidst that uniqueness. It became apparent to me that I had to deepen my fundamental understanding of what it meant to integrate my spirituality and my femininity, to discover what it meant to me to be a spiritually awake woman.

Finding my home in the West once more meant initiating new beginnings to develop a direction and identity that was in rapport with my inner direction and unfoldment. Finding myself leading retreats, establishing a relationship, and bearing my children were all changes that constantly challenged the questions of my identity and the depth of my understanding. They were all lessons in humility, in opening inwardly and outwardly in new ways, and in finding new ways of responding to the changes I was experiencing.

The beginnings we make are always times of upheaval, change, and, often, anxiety. They are turning points, when we leave behind the familiar past and risk the unknown of the present. Beginnings are moments that are pregnant both with fear and with possibility. Beginnings hold within themselves the potential to be moments of great awakening or journeys into darkness. The degree of grace or resistance we bring to our beginnings decrees the degree by which they enrich us.

It is not always easy to bring that quality of grace to beginnings that are imposed upon us. To confront the truth that we cannot control life is to confront pain and anguish. When loss or separation or even disillusionment forces us to make new beginnings, our first reactions are disbelief, anger, and denial. We feel that we are not ready for change, yet the changes that are forced upon us will not wait for our readiness. In our despair, we feel betrayed, and our betrayal often leads us to try to scramble after a fading past. We try to reassemble the broken pieces of our lives into a familiar order, and we cannot accept its impossibility or our loss.

These are crucial and painful moments. We can strive fruitlessly to recover the broken past or creatively open ourselves to the possibilities of the present. We find that we have nothing that we can hold on to, no identity, no security, no direction: we are naked and we are alone. Countless women who have been forced into new beginnings discover that there emerge from within themselves resources of strength and courage in that nakedness.

These resources empower them to discover directions and identities that enrich and fulfill them.

Grace is found in our willingness to open to the present and to the unknown, and to welcome its unfoldment. Our creativity is found in being able to let go of the past without rejection or denial. Grace is found in our capacity to listen inwardly and to trust in that listening. Creativity is found in utilizing the lessons of the past and the possibilities of the present to enrich our inner connectedness and our connectedness with all beings. Our beginnings are rich opportunities for us to attend to inner qualities and resources that have lain dormant or unconscious.

Attending to the emerging of our own spirituality is a crucial beginning for us. We must struggle with letting go of familiar identities and meanings. Exploring the depths of our own consciousness challenges the images we hold of ourselves and the convictions that we have about life. We go from pride and possession to humility and vulnerability. We discover the importance of personal revelation: there truly is no one who can tell us who we are or the meaning of our lives. Instead of the security of seeing ourselves from without, through the eyes of adopted images or roles, we must learn to see from within, through the eyes of our own wisdom and understanding.

It is an inner seeing that calls for new ways of learning as we discover the limitations of our intellect and our conclusions about life and ourselves. We are familiar with seeing and thinking in a linear way, relying upon our intellect to collect data, values, ideas, and images that provide us with ways of defining the world and ourselves. Our definitions are relied upon to give us an illusion of controlling the world and ourselves.

Our "knowing" provides a barrier to protect us from the fear of the unknown. Our illusions are challenged by our questioning and exploration. We begin to see that none of our data, ideas, or conclusions is sacred. Nor are our illusions of control based on anything but our desperate desire to control.

Opening to the inner receptivity of not knowing is opening to learning. To be able to ask the question *Who am I?* without demanding an answer is to begin to open to inner revelation. We are not moved by fear to create yet another adopted identity. We are moved by the yearning to discover an authentic spiritual identity that addresses the totality of our being.

That place of openness and vulnerability is a frightening place to be. There is little certainty or assurance as to what will unfold within. It is also a place of great freedom and wonder: the freedom to explore the dimensions of our own being and our possibilities, the wonder of inner revelation.

We are strengthened in our quest for an authentic way of being and living by listening to the stories of those who share this exploration with us. As we continue to search for spiritual identities and paths that validate us as women, we will be inspired in our search by listening to other women who have developed their spirituality from the integrity of their own experience. This listening can only help us in learning to listen to ourselves.

Throughout history, women have learned about spiritual development through male spiritual teachers. The stories of men's development have been abundantly documented, while the stories of women's spirituality have remained largely unarticulated. The stories we listen to shape our experience, and our experience shapes our reality. In our spiritual lives, we are searching to discover what it means to be a spiritually awake woman, not a disembodied saint. Listening to the stories of others will help us to trust in and to articulate the truths of our own stories.

It was appreciating the value of listening in our own spiritual deepening that inspired me to initiate women's spirituality retreats in North America and England. The validation, nurturing, and strength derived from listening became immediately apparent. When that listening is joined with inner exploration of our own aloneness, a powerful force is created that inspires us to attend wholeheartedly to our spiritual wholeness. We are empowered to articulate and live the truths of our wholeness, an articulation that is crucial to the survival and well-being of our world.

## *Meditation Guidelines* . . .

To undertake a period of meditation is to offer a gift to yourself. It is an act of caring for your own well-being and consciously nurturing inner connection. It is a time of exploring the most intimate relationship in your life: your relationship with yourself. It is helpful to approach these times with deep sensitivity and care, so that they may be times of enrichment.

To sit on a cushion or to close our eyes in Lotus Pose (Padmasana) does not guarantee that we undertake a meditation. It is the measure of consciousness, sensitivity, and clarity we bring to the present moment that creates a meditative time. When you sit down, you may find that your mind is preoccupied with unfinished business or events and plans that have yet to come. Don't be discouraged: let the thoughts be, without judgment, resistance, or indulgence, and they will pass. Let them recede into the background of your awareness, to join the multitude of other sounds you are aware of. Use your awareness of your breath and body to bring yourself into connection with the present moment.

Memories, images, and thoughts may come into your awareness. Some of them may be pleasant: others may be difficult or painful. You may become aware of your mind seeking distractions to be involved with, so as to avoid being with yourself. All that you can do—all that you need to do—is to be present, to embrace all of this with love and gentleness. To return again and again to being with what is in this moment. Try to find the balance between forcing, which breeds only tension, and passivity, which results only in being overwhelmed. This moment and all that it holds is the mirror in which we begin to see ourselves clearly: it is our greatest teacher.

When you end your meditation, slowly expand your awareness to embrace the room you are in, the people you are with. Try not to rush off to begin some new task, but sit quietly for a few moments absorbing the world around you. Let yourself land softly, being aware of the movement of your body as you rise from your sitting posture and the sensation of your feet touching the ground. Bring the same sensitivity you have brought to being with yourself to being with the world. Remember that meditation is not only something that we do. It is a way of being and a way of seeing where there is sensitivity, receptivity, and clarity.

## *Meditation on Aloneness* • • •

Settle yourself in a comfortable posture, and allow your whole body to relax. Use your breath to establish yourself in the present moment. Simply bring your attention to your breath, and connect with its natural rhythm. Without controlling it in any way, let your breath just breathe itself. Just breathe in with sensitivity, and breathe out with sensitivity. If thoughts, memories, or plans arise, just allow them to pass without resistance to them or dwelling upon them. Open yourself to the stillness within you, the still-ness that surrounds you. Just be present, totally consciously present with sensitivity and receptivity in this moment you are experiencing. Allow your-self to settle into this moment, to receive this moment with spaciousness and openness.

When you feel connected with a climate of calmness and stillness within, bring into your awareness a vision of yourself standing alone atop a high hill. See yourself turning around to gaze upon the valleys and hills below you and the hills that surround you. Turn your eyes upward and see the sky above you, the passing clouds, the vastness of the sky. Feel the touch of the wind upon your face, the sun shining on your body, your feet touching the earth beneath you. Take some moments to feel your aloneness.

Let yourself feel the nakedness and the vulnerability of your aloneness. You have left behind the props of your possessions, your roles, the familiar-ity of your environment, and your identity. The sky does not ask you to become anyone or anything. The earth asks of you no assertion of any role or identity. You cannot possess the landscape you see. The sun above you shines equally upon everything it touches: it makes no distinctions, holds no preferences. In the nakedness that is the truth of your life, all that you can do—all that you need to do—is be present, be conscious, and be receptive. Allow yourself to be touched by the elements that embrace you, allow your-self to touch with sensitivity the world that holds you.

Let yourself feel the truth of your vulnerability. We can collect so much armor in our lives—roles, habits, defenses, and possessions. We try to defend ourselves against fear and pain with our armor. Our armor, too, disables our capacity to love, to open, and to receive. We fear aloneness, but intu-itively we know we cannot avoid it. Alone we discover the meaning of our lives. Alone we have to learn some of the hardest lessons in our lives. Alone we discover the inner vision and truths that liberate us. Alone we die.

Let yourself feel your vulnerability, your aloneness. Feel your responses to it. Is it really something to fear? Does your aloneness truly mean discon-nection, alienation, or loneliness? Is your aloneness a place of anxiety and weakness? Let yourself open to whatever feelings arise within you: embrace them with warmth and sensitivity.

As you see yourself standing on the hilltop, let your awareness deepen and become subtler. Feel the life around you, beneath you, above you: the movements of the trees and the clouds, the shadows on the hillsides, the endless changes that signal life, rising and passing. Feel the same changes within you: the rising and passing of your own thoughts and feelings; the birth and death of sensations and responses, constantly changing but held within the vastness of your awareness. As the vastness of your awareness senses the changes around you, and as the vastness of the space around you holds your own changes, open yourself to feeling the transparency of the lines between inner and outer, self and other. Feel the transparency of the lines between aloneness and oneness.

Let your armor fall away. Your roles, your possessions, your identity: none of these is the truth of who you are. None of these can truly describe the vastness of your own being. None of these can describe the truth of your oneness and connectedness with all life. Let yourself just be, without any definition. Feel the fearlessness and the wonder of that being. Feel the oneness, the connectedness that emerges as you free yourself of the personal definitions that divide you from others, that compartmentalize the world into pieces. Feel the oneness that is the truth of your aloneness. Let yourself merge into a sense of being without definition and without separation.

Be present: Be still. Allow the freedom of your aloneness to emerge. Allow the connectedness of aloneness to speak its own truth. Allow the love and compassion of oneness to fill your being.

# Chapter 2
## *Fairy Tales*

W E GROW UP on a diet of fairy tales, absorbing a romantic vision of life. The stories of Snow White, Sleeping Beauty, and Cinderella are incorporated through repetition to become our personal vision of life and the possibilities it holds for us. The host of heroines who perpetuate the conventional myth of womanhood present us with models for our personal goals, choices, and limitations. Our fairy tales give us a ready-made vision and version of what it means to be feminine, a successful woman, and equally send clear warnings of the pitfalls that lie ready to ensnare us in our quest.

Our own life experiences tell us that the land of castles, enchanted forests, and charming princes bears little resemblance to reality. Yet the eternal themes and repeated morals of our fairy tales still tell the story of the secret dreams held in the hearts of many women. Many scoff at and dismiss the messages of our fairy tales. Yet we cannot deny that their very repetition tells us the story of the ideal and, all too often, the story of our lives.

The modern-day Cinderella or Sleeping Beauty still lives, isolated behind her net curtains, despairing in her kitchen, grieving over her lost dreams of fulfillment. Possessing all the trappings of the "successful" woman yet bereft of an authentic identity or freedom, she is doomed to look perpetually outside herself for salvation and for transformation, for the dream of living happily ever after. She cherishes her belief in a magical force outside herself that will deliver this dream. Without it, the vacuum of her life would be too painful to behold.

It is the very vacuum of her life that makes the contemporary Cinderella her own victim. She turns to the endless promises of the television commercials, the fashion industry, the gadgets and props of our culture that tell her they are the path to the end of the rainbow. She endlessly seeks the mythical prince and the fulfillment of her dreams disguised in a myriad of forms from kitchen cleanser to face-lift. The very elusiveness of her fulfillment lends an element of desperation to her search. It also lends the necessary preoccupation that allows her to ignore her inner alienation. With her goals defined for her by our contemporary mythology, she is saved from questioning the authenticity of her identity and life direction.

All our fairy tales feature the heroine, cast in her role because of her innate qualities and characteristics. Our heroine is, of course, beautiful, desirable, and enchanting. Her beauty is the first of her qualities that places her in a precarious position, for it invites jealousy and spite from other women. A clear message our fairy tales spell out is that we need to fear the wiles and motivations of women around us.

The beauty and desirability of our heroine attracts exploitation and abuse because of the envy she inspires. But our mythical heroine possesses qualities that elevate her above the malice and envy directed at her. Invariably, she is gentle, kind, and magnanimous. Her forgiving, selfless, and generous nature means that she can be relied upon to overlook the pettiness and ill will of others. Our heroine is innocent, pure of spirit, without guile. In our admiration of her purity we manage to overlook the fact that she is also unbelievably naive and gullible. Our fairy tales generate the myth that selflessness and magnanimity provide guaranteed protection against antagonism.

The heroine of our fairy tales is essentially unformed, undirected in her life and identity. She is made visible by her dormant innate qualities of goodness and purity. She first appears in a shadow: passive, awaiting rescuing, awaiting awakening. Our mythical heroine is poised on the brink of assuming her true role and identity in life. She waits for something or, most often, someone to rescue and awaken her. It is this external rescue that enables her to assume her true identity where her worth is recognized and, at last, valued.

Luckily for her, the destiny of our heroine is to be rescued. Despite the force of evil and abuse that is directed at her, the very power of her innate feminine qualities of virtue, passivity, and selflessness guarantee her rescue and salvation. Despite the pitfalls in her life that threaten to ensnare her, she triumphs over them, and her assailants are vanquished by the force of her goodness and the power of her rescuer. Inevitably, our heroine is destined to live happily ever after.

Our fairy tales support the conventional female dream of being rescued by a "prince" so that we, too, can live happily ever after. The secret romance we hold in our hearts is the one of being rescued by someone or something outside of ourselves. It is the dream of salvation from our frustration, our despair, and our fear of being alone. It is the dream of finding eternal protection, love, and union in someone else. It is the dream of being unconditionally valued and cherished by another. It is the dream of the final salvation from our doubts in ourselves, our anxieties about our worth. The goal in our fairy tales and our dreams is to live happily ever after, to find the ultimate salvation from fear and alienation. It is repeated endlessly in our culture and our conditioning. It is the eternal myth we digest and absorb.

The path to this goal is portrayed in our fairy tales. We hear the ceaseless messages of the necessity of us being endlessly giving, beautiful, and selfless if we wish to find the fulfillment of our dreams, salvation. We learn through the absorption of our myths that desirability is synonymous with worthiness and goodness synonymous with acceptability. We hear the eternal messages that we are not complete as we are, but that our wholeness is dependent upon being completed by someone or something outside ourselves. We come to believe that our very femininity rests upon our capacity to be defined, made whole by someone or something other than ourselves.

Our lives are enriched by generosity, forgiveness, and magnanimity. It is only when the cultivation of these virtues is motivated by the dream of salvation by someone else that these virtues become problematic. Instead of discovering an identity that is authentic we cultivate an identity that is presentable and acceptable.

Eleanor, after ten years of marriage, found herself abandoned, left by her husband and blamed by her children for the loss of their father. She wept out her confusion, saying, "What did I do wrong? I gave them everything, I gave them my whole life. All I wanted was to be loved."

In being captivated by our myths we learn to wait for rescue and to await fulfillment. We wait to be made whole. We wait for someone or something outside ourselves to transform our lives. Waiting is understood to be integral to the realization of our destiny. The poet Faith Wilding[1] clearly illustrates a woman's sense of waiting for the initiative of another to direct her life:

> Waiting for my breasts to develop
> Waiting to wear a bra

Waiting to menstruate
Waiting for life to begin. Waiting—
Waiting to be somebody
Waiting to get married
Waiting for my wedding day
Waiting for my wedding night
Waiting for the end of the day
Waiting for sleep. Waiting . . .

While in this space of marking time, we need to be occupied with cultivating the virtues of our femininity. These virtues are defined as giving, surrender, selflessness, desirability, and purity. It is by means of cultivating these
qualities that we will become worthy of rescuing. Essentially, we must
endeavor to earn salvation, to become deserving of the identity of a
"princess."

In this endeavor, we learn to look outside ourselves for a definition of
what worthiness is. If we accept that our salvation rests with others, then we
accept, too, the expectations and definitions of others. We learn the importance of becoming different from who we are, of achieving the goals and
images of perfect womanhood. It follows that by achieving these goals and
images of perfection, we will become ripe for completing and awakening.

These themes permeate not only our storybooks and fairy tales, but run
through every area of our culture. Socially, professionally, and spiritually,
we absorb a barrage of expectations, models, and images of who we need
to become to be worthy, fulfilled, and free. Becoming someone, striving for
goals of perfection, and looking outside ourselves for wholeness are messages our society endlessly repeats. We compare ourselves to the messages
and models of perfection we receive and inevitably we find ourselves to be
lacking and inadequate. Nonetheless, all of this striving is seen to be necessary if we are to realize our dream of living happily ever after.

The Cinderella myth has assumed new variations with new expectations
for women as our culture changes. We adopt new models for being and
strive to actualize them in our lives. The "liberated" woman is expected to
pursue a career, while the "superwoman" is expected to handle serenely
both a career and motherhood. The new "super superwoman" has become
the career woman who has realized that the needs of her family are of para-

mount importance and relinquishes her career in order to devote full attention to them. She bears an uncanny resemblance to the original Cinderella.

We may not be looking for the mythical idealized prince to come charg-
ing on his white steed into our lives to offer us salvation. Instead, we may
find ourselves looking for the stamp of approval, affirmation, the confir-
mation of our worth through and from others. We may find ourselves seeking self-definition through that which we win—possessions, accolades, and
roles. We may look for self-definition through being won by someone other
who offers us identity and wholeness.

It's a serious business, this search for perfection. Our salvation as we
know it is at stake. Our rescue and subsequent living happily ever after rest
upon our ability to become worthy to achieve union with our image of perfection, for only then will we be worthy of someone other to save and complete us. Failure, it seems, will doom us to the alleged horrors of aloneness,
eternal spinsterhood, and being "left on the shelf." The threat of these horrors spurs us on in our search for worthiness.

One important step on the path to the state of worthiness is omitted
from our fairy tales. The heroine in our stories is seemingly born into a state
of purity, generosity, and selflessness. By some magical leap she appears to
have bypassed the impurities that assail us. We may admire our heroine and
aspire to her image of perfection yet find ourselves encountering seemingly
endless barriers and obstacles in our path. We find ourselves trying to cope
with our inner fears, anxieties, and lack of trust in ourselves, and our fairy
tales offer few clues as to how to surmount them. The princess within ourselves is all too often overshadowed by the presence of the spiteful sister or
the jealous and petty queen, those assailants who also live within us.

We know deeply and surely that these qualities of our being and their
expression do not attract the stamp of approval from others or from ourselves. We know that the jealousies, the resentments, and the negativities we
find within do not enhance our desirability or merit the stamp of worthiness. Recognizing this and fearing abandonment, we cannot help but feel
that we must aspire to become someone other than who we are if we are to
reach our goal of perfection. Equating our anger and frustrations with
worthlessness, we see them only as a barrier to perfection, qualities to rid
ourselves of. Focusing upon our images of perfection, we try to shed our
"impurities" by suppressing them or trying to overcome, transcend, deny, or

reject them. We are prisoners of our own fiction, believing that these qualities within us prevent us from reaching the "happily ever after" ending.

We appear to have only two options as long as we are captivated by our mythology—to strive for perfection or to sink into passivity. The heroines of our fairy tales earn their salvation simply by enduring the misery inflicted upon them. In choosing the option of passivity we live in hope that the otherness we seek to bring us wholeness and salvation will overlook or ignore the imperfections and weaknesses that are our burden.

Iris Murdoch, novelist and philosopher, once wrote that "the freedom from fantasy is the beginning of human liberation." Women's fantasies have been eternally tied to a romantic fiction where we seek awakening through a combination of striving to become worthy of rescue and then passively awaiting salvation by a person, a role, or an identity, by something other that will complete us and make us whole. The beginning of our own liberation is awakening from the fantasies that limit our lives and bind us to a belief in incompleteness. The most undermining myth we subscribe to is the conviction that wholeness and salvation can only be determined by something or someone outside ourselves, a conviction that leads us to seek wholeness in ways that essentially demean us.

Reflecting on her life, Maria says,

It was dreamlike. I always felt I was reaching for something that was just beyond my grasp, like trying to find an oasis in a desert. I spent years running after things and they were never enough. The problem wasn't that I didn't get them. The problem was that I did get them—success in school, a good career, a marriage with all the props of the "good" life. But I could never stop pushing, trying to prove myself, comparing myself. One day my car broke down and I had to walk, and I was rushing, rushing to get to an appointment and some children on the street saw me and started laughing at me. I went through a whole range of emotion, anger at the children, frustration over my lateness, and finally a real surrender. It was laughable: so uptight, so angry, so affronted by my lack of control over what was happening. So I stopped running. The whole charade of my life felt so incredibly empty. I began to spend more time with myself and stopped filling every blank space in my appointment book. I began to eliminate much that heretofore had seemed indispensable. If I don't have so many "good" things any more, or so many signs of "success," I have myself and I feel rich.

When we are tied to our fictions we look for rescue in places where it cannot be found, we look for wholeness in ways and places that leave us feeling needy, unfulfilled. We reach out to other people, to roles and identities, and to things, seeking an elusive oneness that all too often leaves us feeling only separated and alienated. Cinderella is directing our lives when we find that our need to please others is more significant than our acceptance of ourselves. Our lives are being governed by mythology as long as our identity rests upon the props we are able to accumulate. We are seeking to be the heroine in our own fairy tales as long as we seek sanctuary in the protection of others or in roles. The challenge we face in our lives is to untangle the myths and fictions that bind us if we are to discover an authentic identity and freedom.

The first step in untangling our myths is an unwillingness to settle for sanctuary instead of freedom, an unwillingness to consent to pseudoidentities that offer only limited fulfillment, and an unwillingness to accept that wholeness must lie outside ourselves. We need to be able to discard the messages we receive from our fairy tales and our culture telling us that rebellion against the goals and images of worthiness will mar our femininity and make us less worthy. Carolyn Heilbrun, feminist writer and scholar, succinctly puts it thus: "Fairy tales join the conventional culture in transmitting clear warnings to rebellious females. Rebellion for such a heroine results only in nagging doubts about her femininity and identity."[2]

Our doubts about the truth of our fictions and our "heroine" identities are worthy of honor and respect. This questioning is worthy of nurturing. By doubting, we are no longer tied to these fictions that tell us we are dependent on completion by someone or something outside ourselves. Doubting is the first step in letting go of these fictions. Finding an authentic identity necessitates exploring options and possibilities that are not predetermined by our fairy tales. Karen Rowe describes the tunnel vision from which we suffer when tied to our fictions: "the heroine role in fairy tales dooms female protagonists to pursue adult potentials in one way only: the heroine dreamily anticipates conformity to those predestined roles of wife and mother."[3]

There is fear in setting aside our fictions and myths. Mary E. Giles describes the uncertainties that beset us in *The Feminist Mystic:*

> There are no sure voices to guide us. We listen for them, anxiously, and search the lonely corners of books and churches and, yes, even the minds of friends and teachers, but none echoes the counsel of reassurance for which we yearn. We shake the old order with cries of anger and contempt, demanding its yield of authority and knowledge, but when the words fall, we cover our ears against the shallow ring. We are a present, suspicious of the past, uncertain of the future. We are the women of solitude, being taught the art of living in and through the Spirit, and it is not easy.[4]

Discarding our fiction we are faced with discovering an authentic identity for ourselves. We may find ourselves doubting the validity of the paths that we choose. The familiar signposts of success do not appear in their predictable pattern. We may find ourselves doubting our own capabilities to find wholeness inwardly, feel ill equipped even to know where and how to begin in our quest for completeness. The biggest fear we face is that we will not "live happily ever after," that salvation will be denied to us. If we are overwhelmed by that fear, we will settle for approval, affirmation, and predetermined identities, for this is salvation of a sort—it is a salvation from fear.

The very essence of our being cries out for wholeness, to taste oneness and freedom. It is the voice of the mystic within us. The mystic within seeks the harmony and rapport of oneness, the end of division and falseness. It responds to a vision of life, of being, where there is an end to conflict, prejudice, and superficiality, an end to hatred and resentment. Inwardly, we see a vision of being that is not colored by defense or aggression, where separation ends in wholeness and freedom.

Heeding that inner voice, we are grieved by the way of our world. Its alienation, conflicts, and exploitations wound the very essence of our being. The mystic within knows that there is a way of being, a way of living where there is compassion, love, and joy, and the inner mystic reaches for a taste of that wholeness. A female Native American shaman recently stated, "We live in a way most unnatural to our true selves, and our true selves know this."

The mystic within is handicapped by our fictions and myths, our social and spiritual conditioning. The mystic within is diverted and distracted by the pressure of expectations, spoken or unspoken, imposed or absorbed. We are distracted by fear and primarily by not truly understanding ourselves, our possibilities and potential. In our pursuit of wholeness outside ourselves we devalue, deny, or ignore the tools for awakening that lie within us. We overlook or invalidate the fertility of our own being as a vehicle for awakening. These diversions and distractions are the knots to be untangled if we are to free ourselves of the blinkers of our own fictions. It is an unraveling that allows the mystic within to speak with the voice of freedom, which permits us to define ourselves by our own wholeness and direct our lives with love and truth.

No woman is a consistent paragon of generosity, love, equanimity, and wisdom. The tapestry of our being is woven of many contrasting threads. We experience a range of emotions and qualities emerging within. Our love is contrasted by our grief. Compassion and anger are no strangers each other. Just as we experience the power of connection we experience, too, the pain of isolation. We experience depths of generosity followed by seemingly equal depths of need. We delight in our joy and we despair in our sadness. The contrast within us becomes unacceptable to us when we are swayed by our models of perfection.

The standards of acceptability dispensed by our culture have taught us to call particular qualities within ourselves negative. We equate them with inadequacy and imperfection. Our anger, resentment, grief, and need are seen only to be barriers to our perfection. Instead of discovering oneness within ourselves, we seek oneness in an outer image of personal perfection. Our belief in our inadequacy and incompleteness is translated into need: the need to aspire to our goals of perfection, the need to become someone divorced from who we are.

We find ourselves immersed in a relentless struggle to overcome the "negative" and "unworthy" within ourselves so we can achieve an acceptable, worthy identity. Despising and disliking ourselves, we deny, negate, and undermine ourselves. We reject any expression of ourselves—our sexuality, emotions, needs or aspirations—that fails to conform to our image of perfection. We find successes and we gain respect, approval, and acceptance, yet our gains are so fragile, being based upon denial. Rebukes, disapproval, or negative feedback from others become signals that yet further modification needs to be made within us. The possibilities of becoming are endless. It leaves us with an underlying and undermining sense that we are never quite right, never good enough.

Seeking that point of perfection created by our images is pursuing the mythical gold at the end of the rainbow. It is elusive and yet we interpret our failure to reach it as yet further signs of our inadequacy and incompleteness. We find ourselves bound to this endless wandering in search of our images because we believe that our salvation and wholeness are dependent upon the success of our search. We carry the burdensome conviction that we must become lovable and acceptable to others before we can accept our own worth.

The lessons of childhood are not easily discarded. Conformity, obedience, and "goodness" are abundantly rewarded with praise, love, and acceptance. Disobedience, nonconformity, at times even assertiveness are punished or received in an atmosphere of rigid silence. The voices that govern the pain and elation we experience as children are internalized to become the inner watchdogs we carry through our lives. Praise and acceptance at any price and the avoidance of rejection or blame through any sacrifice become the guidelines that govern our lives.

Sonia describes her life as a performance:

I was a convincing actress as a child, a woman, a wife, and a professional. I knew the right stance to meet everyone's expectations and every situation. I knew when to back down, when to assert, when to use my sexuality, and when to plead my helplessness. I knew how to win, and I knew what I wanted to win. I was liked and admired for my agreeability, and I knew how to avoid threatening anyone. The fact that I couldn't sleep at night without a pill, couldn't live with my tension without a frequent drink or Valium, and couldn't initiate anything without ironclad guarantees of success seemed a small price to pay for the prizes I was getting. I began to realize that I was still performing even when the audience was nonexistent, and I was terrified of my own emptiness. I was a praise addict, an acceptance junkie and I could never get enough. My withdrawal was imposed on me when my husband left me and my smiles and postures got more and more artificial and brittle. I was left with myself, and I learned how to live with my aloneness. I knew the turning point had come when I began to love being alone. I found myself being able to be with people without being a beggar for their love and I wasn't empty. It was when I began to learn that I could say no to other people that I could begin to say yes to myself.[5]

The conventional option offered to women promises wholeness and salvation through bonding with another person. Relationship and marriage sanction our worth and acceptability as a woman. Apart from the social sanctions that are offered, our own life experience tells us of the importance of bonding. Relationships of intimacy offer us the possibility of oneness, releasing our own resources of love enable us to merge with the spirit of another. Our own experience also tells us that when we carry the burden of our fear of aloneness and the belief in our inadequacy into relationship, the oneness we taste is distorted. Too often, instead of merging, we find ourselves submerged.

Because we are alienated from an authentic identity, our definition of ourselves relies primarily upon the way in which others define us. We crave definition to save us from floundering in a twilight of mediocrity. We pay a high price for our craving. We join the ranks of women who promote the virtues of selflessness. It is a tradition with clearly defined rules—preserve harmony at all costs, discard doubt and never be the source of discord. The institution of selflessness decrees that the needs of others are invariably more important than your own, and the aspirations of your partner are consistently more significant than the ones that you hold. Craving acceptance, fearing rejection, we begin to discard our own needs and aspirations to perpetuate the sanctuary of our relationships. Emily Dickinson[6] writes of the effort to numb emotion:

> Me from Myself—to banish—
> Had I Art—
> Impregnable my Fortress
> Unto All Heart—
>
> But since Myself—assault Me—
> How have I peace

Except by subjugating
Consciousness?

And since We're mutual Monarch
How this be
Except by Abdication—
Me—of Me?

Conceptually, we try to convince ourselves that this brand of selflessness is part of relationship. Letting go, surrender, postponement, and deference are what we must give if we are to receive continued affirmation and sanctuary. Sacrifice becomes our rule of being. We face the conflict of discovering that our theories do not fully explain away our feeling of being lessened and demeaned by our sacrifice and surrender. It is not easy to accept that the doctrine of selflessness practiced by countless women throughout history has been and continues to be the major obstacle to their growth and freedom from fear.

We gain through the transactions in our relationships desirable dividends. We are sheltered from the challenge of authentic independence. We gain a sanctioned role and identity. We have a pseudo-oneness and can present to the world an acceptable mode of being. Simone de Beauvoir observes, "Women accept the submissive role to avoid the strain involved in undertaking an authentic existence." Yet we cannot close our ears and hearts to the voices within us that speak to us of the price that we have paid. Again and again, the reality that we are still not living "happily ever after" raises its ugly head. Inwardly, we cannot deny the feelings of neediness and lack of fulfillment that continue to haunt us, and there is never enough proof to assure us of our lovability and worthiness.

Countless women move through life in the darkness of depression, unable to articulate or resolve the discontent they have so capably submerged. Other women find themselves becoming increasingly resentful and demanding as their discontent seeks an outlet. Outer change becomes the way by which we try to solve our problems: getting married or unmarried, changing our jobs, or changing our lifestyles. We ask ourselves if we have not given enough or been loving enough. We attempt to explain away our discontent by proclaiming to ourselves that we have not yet found the "right" man. The oneness we seek continues to be elusive, and, unwilling to confront our self-doubt and self-negation, we maintain sanity only by doubting and negating our partners and life situations.

It is a vicious circle. Our failures in finding wholeness and salvation outside ourselves serve to deepen our lack of trust in our adequacy and inner wholeness. The endless frustrations we experience bring their own messages of doubt in our worth and value. Our fears of dependence and independence, being alone and being in relationship continue to permeate and govern our lives until we are willing to recognize the extent to which we direct our lives from a foundation of fear. That recognition is a turning point, when we no longer lay the burden for self-definition upon others nor pursue empty promises of fulfillment. It is a point not of negation of relationship, but of recognizing that we can only begin to experience mature and free relationships with others when there is a sound and rich inner relationship.

Diane describes her own turning point:

I have been trapped by my own "goodness." I was always "good" in school, in work, and with my husband. I lived to love, to give, to care, and to serve. I was too "good" to be true. I felt guilty about taking anything: praise, time for myself, or the time of others. This surely was selfish, and because I had been schooled in a convent, I deeply believed in the consequences of the sin of selfishness. No one ever told me about the consequences of the sin of self-negation: I discovered them for myself. I erased myself; I was no one, only an extension of others, living for and through them. Attending a spiritual renewal retreat, I couldn't believe how lost I felt. Everyone else seemed at peace, content in their contemplation. I only wanted something to do. The director was wise, refusing my persistent requests to be of service: wash the dishes, help with the meals, anything. She asked me if I knew how to be; I knew only how to be someone or something. I felt cheated, cheated by my own denial of myself, and the camouflage of my "doing" no longer worked. Over the course of the retreat, I began to experience a freedom and a peace that I had always believed was going to come as a reward for my "doing" and it never had.

Disillusioned with our attempts to find oneness externally in the world, we begin to explore the dimensions of spirituality. Perhaps we return to familiar spiritual traditions in the hope of finding new meaning: perhaps we begin to explore contemplative traditions that hold few associations for us. We cannot deny the voice within us that reaches for wholeness. It is a call that has eternally brought people to the contemplative life. But when we begin to explore available traditions and spiritual belief systems we meet some old and familiar acquaintances. The images and models of perfection, the spoken and unspoken expectations of who we must become to be spiritually worthy, await us.

We hear once more the eternal messages—generosity, selflessness, sacrifice, and patience are the tickets to salvation. We hear again that wholeness and salvation exist apart and separate from where we are and who we are. Throughout time, women have cultivated the paths of self-punishment and self-negation and have learned to see such things as virtues. Whether it is the Buddhist nun who patiently awaits the leftovers of the monks, or the contemporary woman in our culture who deprives herself of needed time and personal space in order to be available to others, women have learned to call self-deprivation the path of selflessness. We learn again that oneness will be won through, once more, becoming worthy of salvation. The messages we too often hear reinforce our own conditioning. Once more we find ourselves on the well-traveled path of striving and reaching for wholeness outside ourselves.

I do not question the value of generosity, selflessness, and patience. Our world and our own lives are enriched by their presence. I also do not question the validity of freeing ourselves of patterns of self-destructiveness and self-negation. Our own growth and our capacity to relate to and connect with our world rely upon our nurturing those resources and qualities within us that are life-enhancing. I deeply question the authenticity of the generosity and selflessness we gain when these are products of suppression and the craving for acceptability. I deeply question the authenticity of the inner work we engage in when it is motivated by the desire to conform to a model of perfection, be it a model dispensed by others or one created out of our own conditioning. I challenge the conviction that we must be deemed worthy to discover salvation, and that anyone or anything is qualified to meas-

ure our state of worthiness. I challenge the belief that salvation and wholeness lie outside ourselves and can be won.

Until we confront the belief systems that are founded on fear and a belief
in our incompleteness, our spiritual lives will be yet another backdrop for
our patterns of self-negation and devaluation. In our inner journey and
exploration, we become brutal toward ourselves. We heartlessly use our
new spiritual values to censor and to evaluate our worth. We assume the
stance of watchdog over our own inner life, guarding against the intrusion
of the negative or the weak. We can equally assume a stance of being passive and timid, waiting for someone or something else to deliver salvation
and awakening to us.

Transferring our fear and self-doubt to our spiritual quest, we seek and
create sanctuaries in a person, tradition, or belief system we perceive as
stronger and more worthy than ourselves. In our uncertainty and passivity
we are receptive to, if not inviting of, conversion. We want to belong, we
want to be a part of something larger or stronger than we feel ourselves to
be. We look to an authority to tell us how to be and what to become; we
look once more to models and tradition to define ourselves by.

Leslie describes the spiritual pilgrimage she engaged in:

> I was disillusioned by the West—its values were empty for me—and I
> was disillusioned by the hypocrisy of Christianity as I perceived it. East-
> ern mysticism had always fascinated me, and I held all the usual roman-
> tic fantasies about India. When I was nineteen, I donned my backpack
> and set forth to discover my own enlightenment in India. I looked for
> an ashram, not just any ashram, but a strong and powerful one with a
> magnetic guru. There was no shortage of them, and I was soon estab-
> lished at the feet of a master. I saw that the strength of the ashram was
> equal to the strength of the order that prevailed in it. Everything was
> defined: how we dressed, the way we sat, our free time. There was a
> remarkable sameness: we even spoke the same language, no longer
> using personal pronouns; "one" was the accepted word to define expe-
> rience. We spoke on "one's" impurities and "one's" devotion. Our life
> was spent endeavoring to become the perfect "devotee," because then
> we could be touched by the wisdom and presence of the master. At

some point, I realized that I had exchanged one set of iron chains for another of gold. I was a willing participant in a scenario where I gladly and willingly gave away my freedom. The master whose feet I sat at was never, ever going to invite me to sit beside him, solely because I was a woman. And my wish to do so, I was told, was clearly an expression of my pride and delusion. I left, grateful for the awakening I had received. I awakened to the extent to which I was willing to exchange freedom for security. My disillusionment was a precious gift: it freed me to listen inwardly and begin to grow in a way that felt true and real.

We easily mistake sameness and conformity for oneness and are left unfulfilled and in conflict. The price of belonging is too often a surrender of valid doubts and the freedom to question. Too often, it is a surrender of our own uniqueness and the possibility of fulfilling our potential as a unique and inimitable woman. In our sameness and belonging, we remain alienated from the mystic within ourselves.

We are magnetized by the possibilities that spirituality offers to us. Mystics, throughout time, have spoken of the freedom, wholeness, love, and compassion that is the essence of each of us. The mystic within withstands the detours in our lives that distract us from discovering an authentic wholeness. The mystic within at times expresses herself in discontent, her unwillingness to settle for pseudo-oneness or facades of freedom. It is the voice of the mystic within that empowers us to discard the social and spiritual values that undermine and limit us. At times her voice is only a whisper we can hardly hear, at times she speaks clearly, and at times she grieves. We continue, despite the detours and dead ends, to attend to her voice, for hers is the voice that sings the song of the freedom that is our essence. We heed her voice, for we are desolate without its presence.

It is when we are disconnected from the voice of the inner mystic that our belief in our incompleteness overpowers the intuition that speaks to us of the inner wholeness that lies waiting for us to discover. It is when alienated from the mystic within that our belief in our inadequacy cripples our growth, that our doubt in ourselves undermines our capacity to trust in ourselves. When we are handicapped by our destructive patterns of self-negation, we translate the possibilities that spirituality offers into ideals and models and compare ourselves to those ideals. We then look inwardly and perceive the gap that exists between our ideals and actualities, and the only available option to bridge that gap is perceived as being the bridge of self-negation. What we seek to negate are our apparent "weaknesses" and limitations. Too often, what we seek to negate is ourselves.

The courage to question our models, images, and ideals of perfection is born of pain, disillusionment, and, at times, desperation. At some point, the very elusiveness of the salvation we seek outside ourselves, in and through others, inspires us to question the worth of the success and salvation we have so desperately sought. If we are to reclaim our spiritual heritage, we must willingly take that leap from the known and familiar sanctuaries that have protected *yet also limited* us to experience the unknown. We must be willing to explore the depths of our own being wholeheartedly. It is no path for the spiritually tepid. All we stand to lose are our illusions of safety.

As we begin to heed the voice of the mystic within, we are able to ask the questions that are crucial to our growth and freedom. The wholeness that we seek: does it truly depend upon becoming perfect and worthy of salvation; does it, in truth, involve striving for images and models of perfection? Can the oneness we seek ever be found through defining ourselves by others or through others at all? Achievement relies upon something separate and apart from ourselves to be achieved. In that seeing, we begin to challenge whether wholeness is an object or a state outside ourselves that can be attained, knowing also that it is not an object of mind. The embryo of inner trust is nourished by our questioning. The only way we can begin to discard our myths is by questioning their reality. Questioning is the first and most important step. Inner wisdom begins to emerge when we are no longer distracted by projections that see wholeness and freedom as lying outside ourselves. We begin to trust that all that we need for transformation lies within ourselves and within the present moment.

To abide in inner wholeness calls for the nurturing of immense depths of sensitivity, love, and openheartedness. It is a love that honors the validity of reaching out to others and to our world to form bonds of connectedness. The bonds we form enable us to respect the dignity and spirit of all life. When we no longer demand the returns of salvation and wholeness from our bonds, *our heartfelt connections with all of life serve to enhance our own capacity for love.*

Awakening our innate capacities for love, sensitivity, and open-heartedness, we begin to appreciate the transforming power of love and how integral it is to discovering wholeness and freedom. We are empowered to approach our quest for wholeness with gentleness, rather than with striving or negating. The watchdog and the censor are replaced by a way of being in which we can be a sister, a mother, and a friend to ourselves. An inner environment of open-heartedness emerges in which the inner wars and struggles between the negative and the positive cease without there being either winner or loser.

It is this very climate of love and sensitivity within ourselves that brings transformation. The compulsion to deny or rid ourselves of isolated qualities of our being disappears when we are able to embrace the total tapestry of our being without prejudice or contempt. The degree to which we are able to bond with ourselves in a way that honors our spirit and integrity is the degree to which we are able to bond with all of life. Bonding, and the love it implies, is a prerequisite for transformation.

We are never diminished by giving when we heed the voice of the mystic within, which honors with conviction and certainty the fundamental oneness we share with all beings. Honoring this oneness, there is wisdom in our giving. This giving is essential: without it, we succumb to the pitfalls of passivity, fear, and uncertainty. A wise generosity is knowing deeply and surely what enhances the dignity and spirit of all life and what negates and undermines it. A wise generosity knows not only when to give, but also when to refuse to give.

We need to learn new ways of being generous with our patience, our openness, and our vulnerability. We need to integrate radically new perceptions of how and what to give up. We are lessened and demeaned by the giving or giving up of anything when our giving is born of fear. The giving that is created out of the fear of rejection or abandonment always bears the taint of giving something away, losing ourselves. What we lose in the transaction of giving through fear is our dignity and respect for our own being. It is a giving that leaves us feeling weak and powerless, also resentful and bitter.

The fulfillment of our spirituality calls for surrender, a surrender that is qualitatively different from the one our fairy tales speak of. An authentic spiritual path will never call upon us to surrender our freedom to question, our inner direction, or our inner trust. This surrender belongs to a way of being that only demeans and undermines us. What we need to surrender are our patterns of self-negation and self-denial. We need to surrender our reliance upon others for self-definition and our images and models of perfection. We need to surrender our conditioned ways of seeing that lead us to look to others for salvation and wholeness.

The essential surrender that is called for is the surrender of our fictions and myths that lead us to believe in our incompleteness and inadequacy. We are dignified by this surrender. We are free to turn inward, to trust in ourselves, and to heed the voice of the mystic within, who sings the song of wholeness and freedom.

## *Meditation on Exploring Personal Myth* • • •

Find a quiet place and settle yourself into a comfortable position. Take a few deep breaths, and consciously relax your body. Just stay with the movement of your breath for a few minutes, letting yourself settle into the moment, into being present. Let go of the thoughts and images you are carrying, and just harmonize your attention with your breath. Allow yourself to be still, sensitive, and present.

In that stillness, silently say to yourself, *I am whole. I am free. I am complete.* Just be aware of how your body, mind, and feelings respond to those statements. Do you feel a tightness, a contraction? Do you feel anxiety or inadequacy? Do you feel anger or sadness? Do you feel numbness, a lack of response? Do you feel joy and an echo of affirmation within you? Just give bare attention to your response: feel your response within your body, without judgment or avoidance. Allow your own responses to make themselves felt.

Come back to your breath and to a sense of openness within yourself for a few moments. Reflect on where you are going at this moment in your life, and reflect on the meanings of your life. What are the goals you are moving toward? What do you value, give energy and importance to? What are you trying to move away from, feel fearful of? What are you trying to become? Don't try to find answers or descriptions: just be receptive to whatever responses arise within you in thought, feelings, or body sensations.

Come back to your breath for a few moments. Be aware of any tension or tightness within you. Let yourself settle into the rhythm of your breath, releasing any holding. Reflect for a few moments upon the inner forces that move you in your life. Does fear move you—do you yearn for the approval and acceptance of others? Do you armor yourself against the invasion you feel from the world? Does love move you—do you care for you own well-being and for the well-being of your world? Does anger move you—are you harsh toward yourself or others? Let your responses come without judgment or resistance. Surround your responses not with tension or denial, but with spaciousness and compassion. Be open and honest to and with yourself; be gentle and sensitive. Welcome your responses with warmth and receptivity.

Come back to your breath for a few moments, not holding on to any image or feeling. Be present once more with the tides of your breath; be spacious and open to the moment you are experiencing. Reflect for a few moments upon your vision of yourself. Do you trust that you hold within yourself the potential to be a fully free, sensitive, aware human being? Do you trust that you hold within yourself the needed resources to fulfill the potential you have? Are you connected with your inner resources of energy, vitality, awareness, and wisdom? Are you creatively utilizing the resources you hold, or do they lie dormant within you? Are you waiting for completion, for wholeness? Can you accept that the wholeness you seek lies within you? Let your whole being respond to your reflection, trying not just to *think* of answers.

Once more, attune yourself to the rhythm of your breath, and harmonize yourself with the spaciousness of the moment. Connect with the life and vitality of your breath. Let yourself just be present without trying to become anything or move away from anything. Say to yourself, *I am complete.* Allow it to echo throughout your being. Feel the truth of it. Listen to the wisdom within yourself that affirms it. Say to yourself, *I am free.* Let that statement touch you, letting go of the mythology and images that speak to you of limitation. Filling your entire being with the compassion, awareness, and sensitivity that are rooted within yourself, feel how empowered you are by those resources, empowered to transform your mythology, empowered to abide in the truth of your essential wisdom.

Allow yourself to be still, open, and receptive. In that receptivity, allow yourself to be touched by the truth of your inner freedom. Allow yourself to be touched by the compassion and wisdom within you. All that you can do is be present and receptive. All that you need to do is be present and receptive.

# Chapter 3
## *The Unnatural Divorce*

**M**YSTICS in every spiritual tradition speak at length of the inner freedom that is our spiritual heritage. *Wholeness, oneness, connectedness,* and *awakening* are words used to attempt to describe a dimension of being that is essentially indescribable. They are words to describe a way of living that is an expression of reverence. It is a way of being that reveres the sacredness and dignity of all life, honors our Earth, and appreciates the implications of our fundamental interdependence and interconnectedness. Mystics speak of it as a fundamental inner awakening that empowers us to transform our world.

The language of the mystics has become foreign to us. The words they speak fall on deaf ears. They have become empty of meaning. We know the language of estrangement and separation. *Control, mastery, transcendence, domination,* and *success* are the words we use to describe our experience and our relationship with life. *Power over, isolation, competition,* and *alienation* describe the emptiness of this estranged life.

The path of the mystic is directed toward the end of conflict and suffering. It is the path of honoring the innate dignity and spirit of all life. It is the path of honoring oneness and truth above all else. It is a life committed to peace, harmony, and compassion. The mystic spurns domination and falsehood. She turns aside from exploitation and lives in accord with the oneness she perceives. Above all, she knows the emptiness of the division between inner and outer.

The practice of estrangement is a life without honor. The lines between "inner" and "outer" are clearly defined. Everything "outside" ourselves becomes an object, empty of innate spirit and unworthy of respect. The "outer" becomes subject to the rules of estrangement: objects to dominate, to exploit for our own gratification, to be controlled and subdued.

When estranged, we see the world as empty of spirit. Our response to the world is determined by the possibilities of threat or gratification we perceive in objects. We feel free to exploit the gratifying and to oppress the threatening.

Just as the erasure of the spirit from nature allows the estranged to rape Nature, the erasure of the spirit from human beings becomes the basis for exploitation, genocide, and hatred. Estrangement from the outer world is symptomatic of estrangement from the inner one. War veterans say it was possible for them to destroy the villages of Vietnamese peasants because they were "gooks." White racists exploit people of color because they consider them to be subhuman. Developers feel free to mindlessly abuse our ecology because it is inanimate. Similarly, women have been endlessly subordinated because of their "irrationality" and fundamental inferiority. The language of estrangement deafens our world. All of this represents a disconnection from inner spirit and dignity. The rules of domination and subjugation are applied inwardly to undermine our own well-being and wholeness. Our fairy tales are just one set of such rules. We are strangers to ourselves, divorced from knowing who we are. We become lost in our isolation and experience the effects of our estrangement in despair, alienation, and the paralysis of our creativity.

In our estrangement, we wear the blinkers of isolationism and become ineffective, powerless. We are unwilling to acknowledge that the pain of our world is only an echo of our own pain. We close our ears to the sounds of grief and anguish from the world, for to listen would inevitably be to perceive our connectedness and to respond appropriately. To live in accord with our understanding would imply radical changes in ourselves and in our lives. Perversely, we may be fearful of losing the very isolation that causes us agony. We become fearful of being deprived of our avenues of gratification and fearful of losing control.

Our fear makes withdrawal appear to be an easier option than being awake and connected. Our fear becomes our mantle of protection. It also deadens our capacity to empathize and respond. To acknowledge our connectedness is to feel the pain of the woman who grieves over the death of her starved child, the pain of the woman who weeps over the loss of her dreams and aspirations, and the anguish of the woman betrayed and exploited. The remoteness we experience lies only in the barriers we construct. Hardened to pain, we are equally unreceptive to sharing in the joy of the woman giving birth, the woman rejoicing in her love and creativity.

A dimension of consciousness other than estrangement is possible for us. It is the consciousness of immanence and connectedness. A deep appreciation of the life-destroying consequences of estrangement inspires us to find ways of ending this unnatural divorce from ourselves and others. There are ingredients that are essential to this transformation. Awareness of the necessity and possibility of change is integral to the beginning of change. And I do not use the word *awareness* lightly. Change cannot be born of dullness or apathy! Trust in our own effectiveness is also essential. We need a vision of our own potential for freedom and a vision of how to integrate our understanding of oneness into our relationships, actions, and our very way of being on this Earth.

The degree to which we can connect with our world, empathize, and extend sensitivity rests upon the degree to which we can heal the pain of our divorce from ourselves. Our relationship to our own being is a microcosm of all our relationships. The degree of estrangement we experience inwardly is the extent of our estrangement from others.

Nurturing our own inner awareness is essential to a deepening of our vision of oneness. It is the beginning of our spiritual life. Such nurturing is more than an act of compassion for ourselves: it is an act of compassion toward our world. To learn to connect with and honor our own spirit and dignity is the beginning of learning to honor the spirit and dignity of all life.

Spirituality has frequently been condemned by activists and feminists as being irrelevant, if not contrary, to bringing about needed change. At times, spirituality is condemned as being an escape from and avoidance of issues that "really" matter. Women committed to the spiritual life are sometimes accused of supporting orders and traditions that essentially have only oppressed women and perpetuated estrangement. We need to consider whether these accusations themselves are not rooted in a dualistic way of seeing that separates the spiritual life from the political one.

Aspiring to a vision of connectedness is not a spirituality of narcissism or what some might call a defensive spirituality. The authentic mystic extends herself organically, bringing the light of her integrity into her social, sexual, and political relationships. She does not carry within herself the burdens of artificial boundaries that divorce her spiritual life from her social or political life. Her vision of connectedness and her commitment to the actualization of that vision dissolves the boundaries of estranged seeing. She honors the sanctity of all life and is committed to its dignity.

The authentic mystic knows deeply and surely that, living within her body, she is sexual and honors the expressions of love, joy, and sensitivity that are made possible through her body. She is social and in each moment of her life she interacts with the world around her. She does not ignore a world that suffers and wars, but responds wholeheartedly with her wisdom and love. She is political because she is aware and a conscious participant in life. She is committed to the end of estrangement, which is the doctrine of too many of the structures and value systems that govern our lives. She is contemplative, rejoicing in the richness of her aloneness. She is alone and she is bonded with the world. Her abiding in her vision of connectedness dispels all seeming contradiction.

Although a spiritual quest is a turning inward to nurture awareness and explore the depths of our own consciousness, it is not a turning away from anything. The only valid spirituality is one that touches and illuminates every area of our lives. The "armchair" mystic who observes the struggles of the world from the complacency of her personal achievements pursues a spirituality that is empty of meaning. Suffering, seen from a vision of connectedness, is never an isolated experience. Nor is freedom a personal possession to be gained and hoarded. To commit ourselves in our spirituality to anything other than the end of all suffering and the arising of the freedom and dignity of all life, is to be untrue to the essence of spirituality.

We are easily fascinated and magnetized by the baubles and trophies of the spiritual life. The "mystical" experience, the "spiritual high," "enlightenment," and "transcendence" are concepts that excite us with their promise. When she was traveling the spiritual trail in Thailand, Sheila speaks of how impressed she was with the monastic life:

> Everyone seemed so sincere and graceful. The chanting from the temple, the color of the monks' robes, the silence and dignity of the nuns, the devotion of the lay people all deeply attracted me. I could hardly wait to shave my head, don my whites, and join the community of these enlightened people. The reality of sitting for hours with my legs aching and the sun blasting down on my baldness didn't

quite fulfill my expectations of instant peace and wisdom. Contemplation wasn't always fun. In fact, boredom was initially my predominant experience. I felt resentful and angry when I had to face the reality that *being* enlightened was vastly different from appearing enlightened.

We can be so intent on pursuing the prizes of the spiritual life and, at times, personal glory that we forget that our spiritual insights are liberating only if they are integrated and applied. What value are our highs if we continue to live in an uncreative or insensitive way? What value our "experiences," no matter how impressive, if we still do not know how to live with dignity and compassion? How meaningful are our "spiritual" gains unless they teach us how to end conflict and live with integrity?

When I first began my own spiritual practice in Tibetan Buddhism, I remember how important it seemed to be invited to participate in the "initiations" that were periodically conducted by the senior monks. For each initiation, you were awarded a red string to wear around your neck, and these red strings were interpreted by the Westerners as being marks of spiritual progress. The Westerner walking around sporting layer upon layer of these rather grimy red strings was regarded with awe and admiration. It became something of a life-and-death issue to get those strings. The Tibetan monks never revealed to us whether or not they were laughing up the sleeves of their robes at the files of earnest and pious Westerners lining up for their initiations into the tantric arts. To us it was irrelevant that we neither understood the initiations (not speaking Tibetan) nor that many of us were totally unqualified to participate, lacking the spiritual training that would enable us to fulfill the commitments the initiations called for. What was important was to receive the badges that showed we were going somewhere.

This fascination with the trophies of the spiritual life is probably a necessary stage to go through. We have to be starstruck before we can land with our feet on the Earth. Going from naiveté to reality is as important to our spiritual maturity as going from dullness to awareness.

We live within an undeniable relationship to all life. In every moment of our lives, we influence the quality of the world we live in with our thoughts, feelings, and actions, and, in turn, are influenced by it. It is an inescapable fact of our interdependence with life that just as we are nourished by the world, we also nourish it. This fundamental connectedness means that we cannot, in truth, separate ourselves from anything or anyone. Nurturing awareness of our fundamental connectedness with life, we begin our spiritual quest with a vision that is expansive and holistic.

Love and respect, for ourselves, for all beings, and for the planet we live on, are born of a vision of fundamental connectedness. It is love that impels us to external action, to extend ourselves in a way that is dedicated to the end of conflict. It is love that enables our own spiritual potential to unfold and be expressed fully. When we lack that profound vision of interconnectedness, our lives become dedicated to the pursuit of comfortable isolation, creating a personal and estranged world for ourselves, where the maximum amount of pleasure and gratification is generated and the maximum amount of challenge and pain avoided.

When our quest for the fulfillment of our potential is empty of this vision of connectedness, we create an inner world that is barren, and devoid of the healing and liberating power of love. We inhabit a safe—but desolate— landscape. Our spirituality becomes twisted in a way that perpetuates estrangement and pain. Strangers to ourselves and others, we attempt to create a cocoon of spiritual safety to shelter in.

A woman came to me exhausted by the quality of her life and her intimate relationships. Her home life was a battleground, filled with tension and violence. She was the scapegoat for her husband's and children's suppressed anger. She said, "I desperately need to find some peace, some way of enduring all of this, some calmness. Would you teach me how to meditate?" I gave her some simple methods to enhance her awareness and connect with what she was actually experiencing inwardly. Two weeks later, she returned, absolutely furious with me. She explained that she had followed my instructions diligently, and she was so angry. All she experienced were deep waves of rage and fury for the injustice of her family's treatment of her. She said, "All I wanted was peace, not this awareness that is so disturbing."

It is upsetting for us to discover that the price of safety is, at times, numbness and dullness. It is disturbing to discover that the path of awareness is not always a path of bliss. It is a hard lesson to learn that we cannot bypass who we actually are to gain our spiritual trophies. It is an even more difficult lesson to learn that we cannot ignore the quality of our world nor our relationship with it to gain our spiritual successes. Estranged from a vision of connectedness, we only perpetuate division and conflict.

The fear, born of estrangement, leads us to draw clear lines of division between "me" and "you." Collectively, this becomes the division between "us" and "them." These lines of division are the breeding ground for prejudice, alienation, and exploitation. The unconscious acceptance of this estrangement is experienced inwardly as alienation from our own feelings and potential. Our vision of ourselves becomes dependent upon the material and psychological props that form the boundaries of our personal  worlds. They are the paper houses in which our fragile sense of identity rests. We possess, we believe, and thus we are "someone." We fear the intrusion of anything that threatens our props and belief systems. Our very security and self-worth rely upon remaining unthreatened. The twin tyrants of defensiveness and aggressiveness become the forces that govern our lives and perpetuate our divorce from ourselves.

Spiritual awakening is freeing ourselves from this unnatural divorce from ourselves and our world. But if our spiritual quests are to unfold in a way that awakens us to our connectedness it is essential that the forms and expression of spirituality are free from doctrines of estrangement and false dualities. We cannot divorce the emphasis of the paths we follow from the ends to which we aspire.

A vision of connectedness cannot be born of practices and teachings that, overtly or covertly, emphasize duality and separation. Our visions of spirituality and of our own possibilities are influenced, in subtle and in obvious ways, by the teachings and guidance we absorb. If we are to discover a spiritual vision that is liberating, we need to be willing to question and discard all notions of dualistic seeing and the value systems that perpetuate them.

Few spiritual traditions are willing to confront their prejudices against women. We turn to established traditions in search of paths to the end of estrangement, in search of answers to the questions we hold about the connectedness we sense. In that turning, women meet a wall of cultural conditioning and fear that has been transferred to spirituality. In that transference, age-old prejudice has been accorded a sacred truthfulness.

Having gone to the East to undertake a prolonged retreat in a monastery that emphasized intensive meditation, Andrea was allocated a space on the porch of a building, which she shared with six other women. She was assigned kitchen duties, filtering the drinking water for the monks and cleaning the rice. After participating in the monastery's daily rituals and completing her assigned chores, she usually had an hour or two for her own practice. Worse, this was frequently interrupted by groups of local people who came to gaze upon the unusual phenomenon of a woman engaging in intensive practice. Dispirited, she went to a Western monk to express what seemed to her to be just grievances. The monk regarded her with surprise and proceeded to extol the virtues of her life to her. He said, "I feel you don't really appreciate your good fortune in being here as a woman. You should be grateful for this wonderful opportunity you have to practice humility and selflessness. It's an opportunity that's sadly not available to us monks."

A woman who respects herself and who directs her life to bringing about wholeness and freedom simply cannot establish a spiritual home in any tradition where she is not valued for who she is and what she offers. She is mature enough to know the difference between authentic selflessness and self-negation. She knows that there are many things to be let go of in her quest for freedom, but that inner trust and dignity are not among them.

There are few stories of women's awakening to guide us. Few spiritual traditions are directed by women. Few of the images and models we encounter bear the marks of women. We follow behind the authority figures who define our spirituality and we remain a shadow, if not invisible.

We once spoke in a beseeching voice, begging for the recognition of our worth and spirit. But the tone of our voice is changing. As we acknowledge our own spiritual heritage, we refuse to be cowed or subdued by authorities who refuse to celebrate our spiritual heritage with us. The threats and injunctions that have previously served to quiet our voices are no longer effective.

In the West, the bonding of women strengthens individual women in their quest to reclaim their spiritual heritage. The voices of women in diverse traditions merge to celebrate the discovery of an inner vision of freedom that endures no sanction. The church which has been eternally male-dominated will find itself only male-inhabited if it attempts to continue to justify its refusal to change. In the East and Third World countries, change will be slower as problems of communication and social freedom inhibit the bonding of women. But change will be sure or the monasteries too will find themselves exposed to the need to avail themselves of the opportunity for service and humility by serving themselves.

Our own religious conditioning has bound us to subservient, powerless positions. Simultaneously, it has inhibited our connecting with the voice of the inner mystic, who speaks the truth of our spiritual heritage. We may be courageous in rejecting and discarding any manifestation of prejudice and inequality in our social and professional lives. Yet as novices in our spiritual development, we may be afraid to articulate the doubts and questions that arise in relationship to spiritual conditioning. When accused of pride, or of desiring honor, or of a lack of spiritual depth, we easily begin to doubt the truth of our own doubts.

While we as individuals may be newly awakening to the spiritual significance of connectedness, we need to acknowledge that women as a group are not novices in their spiritual awareness. Women throughout time have shared a common spiritual heritage of connectedness. It is a history that has survived every effort to negate it. Witches, healers, midwives, goddess devotees, and now many contemporary feminists seek to ground their actions, their desires for change, and themselves in a vision of connectedness. In recognizing the truth of connectedness, we are empowered to articulate our doubts and trust in our power to transform ourselves and our world.

Cultural prejudices and dualisms that have been transferred to spirituality will end only when we no longer consent to them. Their continuation can only perpetuate estrangement and dichotomies that are destructive. Men may seem to profit from the dualisms that are promoted, but essentially they are detrimental to both men and women, divorcing both from the connectedness they share.

One such policy of estrangement has become the fundamental teaching of many spiritual traditions and belief systems. It is the dichotomy of "spiritual" versus "worldly." In it, the "inner" and the "outer," "humankind" and "nature" are polarized and specific values are attributed to them. The spiritual life is deemed to be strived for, while the worldly life is decreed to be inferior, to be transcended. Humankind is considered to be of primary significance; nature is valued only for its capacity to serve us. The inner is considered sacred and the outer of doubtful value.

What is this worldly life—so easily dismissed—composed of? Bonding and caring for one another, generating life, directing and creating our social and political lives with sensitivity and wisdom, and rejoicing and despairing with others—this is the worldly life that is held in contempt. Have we considered what the outer is that is so glibly disregarded in pursuit of the sacred inner? It is the life and spirit of our planet, and the degree of struggle and suffering experienced by those we share our planet with. Do we honor the interdependence that exists between ourselves and our planet when we divorce ourselves from the nature that supports and nurtures us?

We live in a world of immense suffering and struggle, and the divorce of spirituality from the world has not contributed to bringing about the end of the violence and alienation that characterize it. Spiritual growth must open our eyes and our hearts. Solomon Ibn Gavirol, the Jewish-Arabic poet and philosopher of Islamic Spain, wisely says, "Of what avail the open eye if our hearts are blind?" To withdraw from the world, to practice a path of estrangement, is life-denying and a negation of the essence of spirituality, which is to end pain. Passive negation and withdrawal degenerate into rejection and denial. A spiritual acolyte once said to me, "I used to feel guilty about my lack of commitment to social and political change. Now that I have deepened my spiritual commitment, I see that I can't do anything about the karma of the world. It's more important to seek my own enlightenment." This same person felt herself to be practicing boundless joy and compassion for all beings. Even if this is true, it is apparent to me that our world is desperately in need of far fewer closet Buddhas.

We need to consider what we lose in the practice of estrangement. The capacity to be touched by and empathize with one another is sacrificed. In closing our hearts to the world, we also close our hearts to the richness of our own love and compassion. Lost in our estrangement, we deprive ourselves of the opportunity to be enriched by the very grist of life. A vision of immanence and connectedness dissolves the constructed boundaries between inner and outer. The understanding that the inner is the outer and the outer is the inner transforms our psyche.

 A spiritual path lies not in any specific mode of existence, but in the openness of appreciating the spiritual potential of each moment. Within the symphony of our being, we hear the sounds of both harmony and disharmony. With a consciousness of connectedness, we can embrace the array of sounds within us, learn from them, and utilize the possibilities for understanding they offer. With a consciousness of estrangement, we polarize the variety of voices we hear. Inner fragmentation begins. We superimpose our values of superior and inferior upon qualities within ourselves. We try to control, subdue, or negate the inferior while pursuing the profitability of the superior.

The dualities we project on to the world are but reflections of deeply rooted dualities that exist within ourselves. There are clear links between the contempt in which we hold nature and the contempt in which we hold our own bodies. The destructive value systems that define our bodies and sexuality as being sinful and worthless are externalized. They become associated with nature and all form in order to justify the abuse of both.

We are not born into this world in neatly compartmentalized packages labeled Mind, Body, and Emotion. We are born as integral, if immature, individuals. Our growth and the expanding of our awareness entails gaining new skills and knowledge that are liberating. It also entails accumulating prejudices and conditioned values about ourselves that are fragmenting.

Absorbing cultural prejudices, we become divorced from the spirit and value of our own bodies. We learn to be secretive about and ashamed of our bodies and their functions. Yet we learn, too, the importance of appearing to be pretty and desirable. Our sexuality matures and we learn to call its expression a curse. Yet we learn, too, that our sexuality attracts interest and affection. Our bodies are our first home, yet it is so difficult to feel at ease within them, burdened as we are by the conflicting messages we receive about them.

We carry with us the traumas of our childhood and adolescence experienced in relationship to our bodies: too thin, too fat; too flat-chested, too big-breasted; too tall, too short; we are rarely, if ever, acceptable to ourselves. We are ridiculed or approved of on the basis of our appearance, and we learn that our bodies are our tickets to approval or rejection. We are either loved or lonely depending upon the appearance of our bodies, which we are unable to control fully, despite our contortions.

Learning that love is seemingly won through our desirability, we endeavor to turn ourselves into attractive ornaments in the marketplace of relationship. The god of desirability is difficult to please. To earn acceptance, we engage in endless occupations to mold ourselves into models of desirability. The "mirror-hours" that women have collectively put in hold sufficient energy to change the world. Instead, they have generated only endless frustration and self-negation.

A woman may find some measure of success in modifying her body to conform to current standards of desirability, only to discover that this, in turn, is interpreted as an invitation to violate by those whom she wanted to please. Exploitation and rape are dismissed because, after all, she asked for it. We blame ourselves for the violations we suffer or remain silent for fear of being blamed by others. This willingness to accept blame underlines the shame we feel in our own bodies. We feel guilty about presenting ourselves in ways that we are trained and expected to do by our culture. Women, estranged from the dignity of their own bodies, collaborate in the social expectations to display their desirability to win affection. Too often, all that is won is the identity of being a trophy possessed by another.

Behind the scenes of all these exchanges there lurk the age-old and deeply rooted messages that essentially our bodies are impure and shameful, our sexuality is sinful, and our femininity a temptation to be conquered. The impressions upon our consciousness based upon the messages we receive and absorb are undermining and destructive.

We internalize the feedback we receive from other people, we absorb the social expectations, and we learn to be manipulative, passive, dependent, and competitive. We become further estranged from our innate dignity and integrity. Our inner sense of respect, trust, and worth is undermined, if not entirely suffocated, and we begin to exist only for others. Fiona speaks of the role her relationship played in the process of negating herself:

I was born with the burden of prettiness. I was the epitome of the beautiful child: blonde ringlets, long eyelashes, and an enticing smile. My parents called me their princess and loved to show me off to whoever would look. They were so proud of me. I was the living proof of their ability to produce perfection. I was never dirty: in school, I never participated in anything that would mar the perfection of my clothes. I was a china doll.

It didn't change as I grew up. I was the envy of all the other girls, and the boys gathered around me like bees to honey. My prettiness guaranteed recognition and praise, from being the teacher's pet to someone everyone wanted for their best friend. I was in love with my own popularity. When my women friends began to be interested in the feminist movement, I dismissed them as man-haters. I couldn't join them because my whole life revolved around the admiration by and pursuit of men. When I was thirty, I got breast cancer, and my whole world fell apart. I felt suicidal after my mastectomy. It wasn't just my body that was scarred: I felt totally worthless. It was a slow path to being healed. I can look in the mirror now with my eyes open, and I see more than the outer scars on my body. Do you know I have even learned to love and respect myself?

The very first step toward ending estrangement is reclaiming our bodies. We do not need to flee our bodies to pursue our spirit. Rather, we need to honor our spirit within our bodies. To be a disembodied spirit negates a human spirituality. We must not live just enduring our bodies, but within our bodies, caring for and honoring them as the visible expression of our spirituality.

Learning to value everything about being a woman is the key to a connected spirituality. The reconciliation between body and spirit is the key to the reconciliation of humankind and nature. Our bodies are neither weapons to be used to win approval nor tickets to acceptance and affirmation. The very rhythms of our bodies celebrate the rhythms of nature, the seasons of our bodies are the seasons of our world. When we abandon our prejudices, we become intimate with the fundamental and intuitive responses of our bodies. A nursing mother may sometimes lactate at the sound of a suffering animal, our hearts open with compassion in response to pain, and our bodies quicken in joy at the sound of a delighted child. In listening to the sounds and responses of our own bodies, we listen to life and there is rapport and connectedness in that listening. "Every act and gesture is a word spoken. We are not overspiritualizing our view of sex when we say that every sexual act, feeling, or emotion has the power to become a disclosure of spirit to spirit. Sexuality is never something by itself. It is always meaning incarnate."[1]

As a vehicle for the expression of sensitivity and love, inwardly and outwardly, we cannot treasure the wisdom of our bodies too much. As long as we are dispossessed from our own bodies, we establish our sense of identity in the expectations of others. The divorce from our bodies, with its ensuing conflicts, is reflected in separation and alienation from other people and the world we share. The resolution of this conflict can only be in learning new ways of relating to ourselves, based not upon prejudice or conditioned values, but upon self-knowledge and inner connection.

Historically, spirituality has actively participated in the prejudice against and rejection of the body. In certain established religious traditions, women are made invisible, swathed in voluminous uniforms to protect both themselves and others from temptation and desire. Our own confused relationship with our bodies is reinforced through the reminder that it was through our bodies, our sexuality, that there was banishment from paradise. There are theologians aplenty to remind us, "You are the door of Satan; you are the one that yielded to the temptation of the tree; you are the first deserter of the law of God; you persuaded man whom Satan himself had not the power to subdue; with irresponsibility you led man, the image of God, astray!"[2]

We learn that our bodies, our tickets to success in social prestige and acceptability, are not our tickets to salvation, but its opposite. Our own history of despising our bodies is matched by the contempt in which traditional spirituality holds the body. In the Buddhist tradition, reflection is encouraged upon the inherent impurity and loathsomeness of the body. Detachment from our bodies is to be cultivated, lest we fall prey to the snares of our sexuality. The degeneration of this detachment is underlined by the story of a mother who traveled halfway around the world to visit her son, living as a monk in Thailand, whom she had not seen for several years. She was not permitted to embrace him and express her joy in seeing him because it offended the vows he had taken. Vows meant to constrain passion equally constrained all physical expression of love.

Our bodies are despised because they are the vessels of our sexuality. Our sexuality is perceived as a power we need to subdue lest it overwhelm our rationality and reason. Our bodies become the scapegoats for our fear of sexuality, and in our fear, we attempt to control them, dismiss them, and suppress them. In our pursuit of a disembodied spirituality, our bodies become regarded as sources of attachment and temptation and our spiritual success is measured by our capacity to renounce, overcome, and transcend them. The destructiveness to women born of this distorted relationship to the body is apparent and is perpetuated in estranged spirituality.

Radical mystics of the past and present have consistently challenged the divorce of the spirit from our bodies and sexuality. In *What Is Love?*, Jules Toner describes a vision of a connected spirituality: "When we love we are present to the beloved and they, present to us, in coexistence, physically, intellectually, spiritually, with affection and passion as co-forms of presence."[3] The weight of our guilt and conditioning overrides the messages of oneness, both outer and inner, that mystics speak of.

In estranged spirituality, the obstacle of the body is renamed and misnamed the obstacle of "woman." Carrying the blame for original sin, woman is to be punished eternally by being banished from any authentic form of acknowledgment by, or participation in, established religion. Women are punished for their weakness by exploitation and oppression. The symbol of the temptress Eve permeates our culture, a living symbol repeated in the media, in literature, and in religious teaching.

The Buddha offered new possibilities of liberation to women in teaching a spiritual vision that offered freedom to all beings. Yet despite his original teaching, the taints of estranged values crept in to distort Buddhism.[4] A dialogue attributed doubtfully to the Buddha defines the relationship of monks to women. The promoted attitude was as follows:

"How are we to conduct ourselves, Lord, with regard to
   womankind?"
"As if not seeing them, Ananda."
"But if we should see them, what are we to do?"
"Do not talk, Ananda."
"But if they should speak to us, Lord, what should we do?"
"Keep awake, Ananda."

The important point here is not whether the Buddha actually made this statement or whether it was made by a later misogynist and attributed to the Buddha. It is that such statements are sufficiently believed in to form the basis of prevailing attitudes toward women.

Women become the scapegoats for the inability to relate to the body and to sexuality with respect and sensitivity. Internalizing the messages received through social and spiritual values, women learn to belittle their spiritual potential. They adopt a stance of passivity, accepting the spiritual banishment decreed to them, regarding themselves as inferior and unworthy spiritual beings, exiled from an authentic spiritual fulfillment. Is it then any surprise that in Eastern Buddhist countries it is a commonly held belief that a woman must wait to be reborn as a man before she can attain enlightenment? She is, meanwhile, encouraged to work toward this worthy goal by accumulating merit through serving with selflessness and humility the patriarchal structure.

I remember the elation I felt when, during my own practice in the East, I was praised for the consistency and intensity of my practice. I remember the horror and despair I felt when the same praise was tempered by the monk's words of regret: "It's really a shame you had the misfortune to be born a woman. But you can feel glad because your dedication to your meditation will surely give you enough merit so you don't have a lower rebirth next time. You're sure to be born in a place where you have the opportunity to become a monk."

The estrangement from our bodies becomes the basis for rejecting life. It separates us from nature and the communion and bonding with others that our hearts yearn for. We learn to feel guilty about our need for connection and misname it spiritual weakness. The yearning to bear and nurture our children, to care for our planet, and to creatively establish our relationship with it are perceived as worldly attachments. In our estrangement, we attempt to subdue them. Through our denial, we come to inhabit an inner landscape that is barren and heartless. We become frustrated and brutal toward ourselves in our suppression of our yearnings for connectedness. This inner brutality and frustration is then projected outwardly in aggression, and in rejection and denial of our world.

A spirituality that embraces our bodies and sexuality is not a narcissistic indulgence in these things, but a celebration of their power to form bonds of communion and connection with all life. Exorcising our feelings of guilt, shame, and inferiority opens the door to establishing a relationship with our bodies—and, indeed, with all the varied manifestations of life—that is creative, appreciative, and loving. Healing our divided selves is born of deep insight, an inner seeing in which there is no rejection or denial, but an appreciation that our bodies are vehicles for learning, understanding, and sensitivity. Rejection is no less a hindrance to spiritual growth than neurotic attachment. Aversion is no less a hindrance than clinging. Banishing the alien presence of prejudice from our own psyche, we can reclaim our bodies and nurture and appreciate their power as vehicles of love and compassion.

Instructed to develop detachment from her body because it was impure, decaying, and unable to bring forth anything of beauty, Sara felt sure enough of her own experience and conviction to be able to challenge her teacher. She denied this myth, saying, "You have missed a great deal in life. So much of beauty has been born of my body. Their names are Joseph, Serene, and Katherine."

A fundamental step in nurturing a spirituality of connectedness is establishing a rapport and reconciliation among the variety of inner dynamics that make each of us a unique and whole individual. In a belief in estrangement, we divorce ourselves from nature. We divorce our spirit from our body and this process of inner fragmentation is supported by our distorted value systems. The process of fragmentation has its own momentum and continues. We create yet further divisions between our mind and our emotions, and between our intellect and our capacity to feel. Calling upon familiar value systems to support this unnatural divorce, we strengthen the divisions within us.

Our minds are seen to be the receptacles of wisdom, the owners of understanding: reasonable, strong, and reliable. Emotion is deemed to be irrational, weak, and untrustworthy. Emotion is attributed to the heart, and reason to the mind; the heart is defined as feminine, and the mind as masculine; the feminine as weak, and the masculine as strong. We are encouraged in our culture to cultivate the power of our minds. The achievement of the goals that our society deems to be worthy relies upon the capacity to evaluate, to be rational and strong in our intellect. We are equally encouraged to dismiss, suppress, or simply "get over" the emotions we experience. But the presence and influence of our emotions are a powerful dynamic that cannot be ignored. Meister Eckhart, a fifteenth-century mystic, touches upon the destructiveness of this belief in disregarding the relevance of emotions:

> For all the truth the authorities ever learned by their own intelligence and understanding, or ever shall learn up to the last of days, they never got the least part of the knowledge that is in the core. Let it be called ignorance or want of knowledge, still it has more in it than all wisdom

and all knowledge without it, for this outward ignorance lures and draws you away from things you know about and even from yourself.[5]

The effects on an individual and global level born of this negation and dismissal of emotion are apparent. Suppression, oppression, aggression, alienation, exploitation, psychosomatic illness, and psychological imbalance are rampant in our world. We wreak havoc and destruction upon ourselves and our world through the estrangements we believe in.

Imbalance is created within the psyche of each individual who bears the prejudice of these divisions. It is an imbalance that governs our relationship with all life. The healing of the world we live in begins with the healing of the imbalances we carry within ourselves. It is not enough to worship the god of reason or the goddess of feeling. There needs to be an authentic reconciliation among the variety of dynamics we experience. To experience the interrelatedness of our inner dynamics is to experience a harmony and rapport that enriches every area of our lives.

All that we truly need for this transformation lies within ourselves and within the present moment. Spiritual fulfillment relies not upon the rejection or denial of anything, but upon the discarding of prejudice and destructive belief systems. The myth of estrangement relies upon fear and denial. The unnatural divorces we endure rely upon the ignorance of our fundamental connectedness. The eternal alimony we pay for this estrangement is suffering and pain.

An integral step in the unfolding of connectedness is the willingness to question all forms of prejudice and the courage to discard them. That questioning allows us to meet ourselves, our entire selves, not through the filters of conditioned value systems, but with eyes that seek only the truth. Only dedication to that which is true will liberate us. A true spirituality is revolutionary in that it supports no falsehood. The falseness of estrangement in all its dimensions is revealed through our own dedication to truth and freedom. Abiding in a vision of connectedness, we abide with integrity, dignity, and love. We are spiritual, social, and political, for our connectedness recognizes no boundaries.

## *Meditation on Oneness* . . .

Settle into a comfortable position, and allow your eyes to close. Let your attention move through your body, relaxing and letting go of any tension or holding that you sense. Just be aware of the stillness of your body, and allow your whole being to merge into that stillness.

Bring your attention to your breath, simply being aware of the whole movement of your breath from its beginning to its end. Let your breath find its own rhythm and depth: do not control it in any way. Allow yourself to trust in the rhythm of your breath, allowing your breath just to breathe itself. Let go of any inner voices that censor your breathing with messages of your breath not being full enough or tense. Let your breath find its own way in your body.

Be aware of the qualitative difference between *watching* your breath and *feeling* your breath in your body. Feel your breath in your body, and feel your body responding to your breath. Feel the expansion and contraction of your body with each breath, receiving with your awareness the movement of life within your body. Allowing yourself to merge in oneness with your breath, breathe in with sensitivity, and breathe out with sensitivity; breathe in with receptivity, and breathe out with receptivity.

As you merge yourself in harmony with your breath, allow yourself to feel the pulse of your life in your breath; feel the pulse of all life within your breath. Feel yourself being nourished by the world with each incoming breath; feel yourself nourishing the world with each breath you release.

Begin to open your attention in order to be aware of your whole body. Beginning at the top of your head, gently and slowly move your attention down through your whole body, touching with sensitivity every area of your body with your attention. Free of resistance or holding, simply open yourself to feeling the different sensations that arise and pass in your body, touching equally with your attention areas of your body that offer no sensation and cultivating an unconditional openness and sensitivity to your body as it is in this moment. Embrace your body with a gentle, loving attention. No need to label your body or any sensation that arises in your body: the body has no label or judgment. Allow yourself to merge, to be one with the sensations in your body as they arise. Just continue that receptive movement of attention down through your entire body.

Be aware that as you connect with the life of your own body, you connect with all life; as you are at one with your own body, you are at one with all of life. Just as your body asks you to answer its needs for sensitivity, for nourishment, for warmth, and for care, all of life is nurtured by that same care and sensitivity. The yearnings of your body to be free from harm and pain are yearnings that you share with all of life.

Being still within your body, feeling the waxing and waning of life as it expresses itself in sensation, just open yourself to being present with your body. Allow that openness and receptivity to embrace the different thoughts, images, memories, and plans that arise in your consciousness. Be aware of how you move toward or away from the different thoughts and feelings that arise. Allow them to arise and to pass without prejudice, without control, and without any judgment. Be aware not only of the thoughts but the space between the thoughts. Be aware of the space that holds your thoughts and feelings, and merge with the openness and vastness of that space.

As you feel that spaciousness within, all that you need to do is listen, with receptivity and with softness. Assume no stance of judgment, of being for or against. Strive for no models or goals. Just allow yourself to be present and to listen inwardly. Merging your whole being into that stillness of receptivity, let the present moment and all that it embraces unfold.

In that spaciousness and stillness, be aware of the transparency of the line between inner and outer. The stillness and spaciousness you feel within surrounds you and holds you. It is not separate from movement or sound: it is in and through all movement and sound. In this moment, you connect with what is held in all of time, past, present, and future. In the life you feel in your breath is held all of life. The sensations you feel mirror the sensations of the universe. Just allow yourself to be still: the interconnectedness you experience is the thread of interconnectedness that bonds all of life.

As you listen inwardly, the thoughts and feelings you receive mirror all thought and feeling. The sorrow you feel mirrors the sorrow of countless generations of life. The joy you feel is echoed in the hearts of all life when there is freedom from pain and fear. The grief you experience in loss and separation is shared by the world. The love that nourishes you nourishes the universe.

Simply be present and listen. Be gentle in that stillness, and know the strength and openness of connectedness, of oneness.

# Chapter 4
## *Untying the Knots*

COMING TO INNER wholeness is, to me, the essence of the spiritual life. But just what is this inner wholeness? By inner wholeness, I mean to convey a way of being inwardly in which we are clearly connected with our own resources of power and strength and understanding. True inner wholeness allows us to live in a way in which we can rely upon these resources and yet have a corresponding openness and sensitivity to the challenges and messages that life can bring us.

Inner freedom—and the capacity to actualize this freedom outwardly—is the essence of spirituality. This freedom is not, however, a state to be achieved: it is not a goal to be attained. Rather, it is a way of being inwardly, which is awakened out of its dormant state by our untying the knots that limit and distort our vision of who we are.

Look at some of those knots. What are the knots that limit us? What are the knots that confuse or restrict us? Certainly there are the knots of mistaken images and identities. The knots of fear, insecurity, and anxiety lead us to create false images and descriptions of ourselves that we believe in. The knots that are destructive lie in underlying conditioned patterns of being that repeat themselves in our lives, and that distort our relationships with others and with ourselves. The knots of opinions and standpoints lead us to erect barriers, defenses to hide behind and also serve to divide ourselves from others. The primary knot lies not only in the contents of our minds or in our conditioning, but also in our belief that all of this is the truth, the reality of who we are. Many of the knots that entangle us can be traced to the conditioning to which we are exposed from the moment of our birth. Some of the conditioning we experience is imposed, thrust upon us. Some of it we have adopted willingly. Conditioned ways of seeing can also be based upon our own life experience and inner experience. All of this conditioning leads us to see life and ourselves in ways that are rigid, static. Our conditioning is the filter that distorts our inner and outer vision. The rigid and fixed ways of perceiving that we adopt govern our relationships to our life directions, other people, and ourselves.

Conditioning is something that each of us experiences. It arises through an experience, interaction, or contact that makes a deep impression upon our consciousness. The impression may be painful or pleasant, but it is powerful, because it becomes integrated, locked into our consciousness to influence our very way of seeing.

It is upon the basis of our personal conditioning that each of us constructs our personal reality. We construct our views and opinions. We construct our attitudes and identities. We construct our images of ourselves and other people. Through the influence of our personal conditioning, we find ourselves striving for particular goals in life and avoiding others. We find ourselves adopting specific roles and identities and disdaining others. Through the bias of our conditioning, we value specific achievements and directions as being worthwhile and significant, and discard others as being empty of value. Each aspect of our conditioning is like a building block we use to construct the house in which we live. Because of the differences in our conditioning, we each inhabit what would seem to be a very different house.

The scientist who seeks to master matter and manipulate our planet inhabits a house very different from that of the ecologist who commits herself to saving the rainforest. The extrovert who communicates easily and surrounds himself with friends moves in a different world from the introvert who moves through life frightened of contact with others. The psychiatrist who labels a hallucinating, unpredictable person schizophrenic inhabits a different personal reality from a psychic who deems the same patient holy. The suburban executive holds a different vision of herself and life than the ghetto inhabitant.

Our conditioning not only influences our life directions and choices, but also clearly influences our capacity to actually fulfill them. The self-image we hold, whether negative or positive, is rooted in our conditioning. It is obvious that our self-image is directly related to the ways in which we utilize our own resources, whether creatively and dynamically or destructively and passively.

Emma was raised in a family who regarded professional success as the ultimate goal to strive for. Her parents made sacrifices and saved in order to give their children a college education and all the good things of life. A good school, pediatrician, and orthodontist, plus a comfortable home ensured that she was well prepared to assume her rightful place in life. Emma was reared in a value system she internalized as her own. Success was the sanctioned goal to aspire to, and success was equated with having, gaining, winning, and securing. The underlying purpose of this success was essentially to enable her to be "someone" and also to be better than others. Confident, assured of her abilities, she proceeded to travel the path that had been defined for her and that she adopted as being worthy. Her dream became her reality and was perpetuated as she raised her children to follow in her footsteps.

Mary's experience of life and vision of herself was very different from Emma's. The youngest child of the family, with two older brothers, she held no high expectations. She was subject to criticism and ridicule. Her brothers' needs and aspirations were always considered more important than her own. They received the approval, the big allowances, the freedom, and the encouragement. She perceived the world as essentially hostile and herself as weak, powerless. She scraped through school, and she continued to live with her parents while holding a low-paying job until she married a man who wanted a wife at home to look after his needs.

One aspect of conditioning that is apparent to us is its pervasiveness. The degree of influence that our conditioning has upon us is directly related to our own degree of awareness of it. If we flounder in dullness or apathy, we are not even aware that our conditioning *is* conditioning. For us, it is the truth. Paralyzed by indifference and lethargy, we are simply overwhelmed by the impressions we receive and the conditioning we absorb.

Whether we are able to learn and grow through the impressions we are exposed to or whether we are simply molded and overwhelmed by them, is determined by our willingness to question and explore the meaning of those impressions. When the rigidity of our conditioning goes unquestioned, it prevents openness, change, and learning. Our static ways of seeing ourselves suffocate our potential to be whole and free. Our belief in our conditioning is a belief in limitation and incompleteness. Locked into negative self-images, our belief in our conditioning as being the truth is stronger than any trust we have in our potential to be free and whole. But when we are encouraged by the support of others and our own divine discontent, we are

inspired to deeply and intimately explore and question our own conditioning and the impact of its negativity upon us.

Another aspect of our conditioning we begin to appreciate as we explore
its depths is the power that it holds to imprison us. We may find ourselves
rebelling and straining against the reins of our conditioning and making resolutions to change ourselves. We experience deep frustration when the
number of resolutions we make is matched by the number of times we fail
to sustain our resolutions. In our relationships with other people, we find
ourselves enacting patterns of communication that fill us with despair and,
at times, disgust, and we resolve to change them. Our despair is deepened
by the seeming powerlessness we experience in bringing about the changes
we desire.

Part of Christine's job as a social worker involved participating in team
meetings to plan policy, distribute caseloads, and so on. She spent most of
her time in the meetings either constantly deferring to her colleagues or
remaining silent in the back row. Outwardly agreeable and docile, she would
leave the meetings bursting with the tension of all the unspoken objections
and disagreements she had been unable to voice. Time after time, she
resolved to go just once into a meeting and voice what she actually felt.
Time after time, she assumed her timid-mouse role in the meeting.

So many of us cherish dreams of aspirations we would like to fulfill, yet
which we have never explored. Tamar had always wanted to paint. But the
cautions of her parents and peers to be sensible and find a steady job were
internalized. Instead, she went from secretarial school to a typing pool. Her
creative dreams were limited to the occasional doodle on scrap paper over
lunch. The gap between her inner aspirations and her actuality widened to
the point that she dismissed her creative yearnings as childish dreams.

Resolutions, willpower, and suppression are avenues unable to bring
about the end of conditioning. Neither is conditioning a force that can be
erased from our consciousness. In fact, it is not even necessary to try to
erase the endless depths of conditioning we have absorbed. Our conditioning is neutralized by the deepening of our awareness. By trusting in our
own resources of understanding, energy, and insight, we have access to the
power to go beyond the boundaries of our conditioning. We begin naturally to explore the depths and possibilities of our own being. Limitation is
the basic expression of negative conditioning. Limits are imposed through

our belief in them. We are effectively blinded to a vision of our own potential through creating truth out of untruth.

The most powerful expression of conditioning that permeates our entire lives is the images we construct of who we are. We rarely know who we are. Instead, we know who we believe ourselves to be. Our beliefs are constructed through isolating particular qualities within ourselves and perceiving those qualities to be a total and true description of our own being.

We perceive the emotion of fear repeating itself in our lives. Highlighting this one emotion and ignoring the rest, we conclude that we are fearful, defensive people. We dislike and feel ashamed of the feelings of envy we experience. Yet our very resistance emphasizes this aspect of our being, and we believe ourselves to be petty, jealous individuals. By isolating and dwelling upon specific characteristics within ourselves, we construct a self-image that becomes a personal reality. We find ourselves either enacting our image of ourselves or trying to compensate for it. The person locked into his or her fearful image goes through life assuming roles, identities, and stances that offer little threat or challenge. Perhaps to compensate for the fear such a person feels, he or she may assume inflated roles of superiority. A woman carrying her belief in and shame over her envy of others becomes endlessly flattering and admiring of others in an attempt to convince herself (and others) that she is free from it. Alternatively, overwhelmed by her envy, she may forever be comparing herself with others.

Locked into our limited images of who we are, we are also limited in our capacity to utilize our inner resources. Above all, defending our self-images or striving to compensate for them drains our energy. This is very important to see. Being focused upon either trying to disguise ourselves because we feel we are inadequate or trying to prove ourselves becomes such an absorbing pursuit that we are left depleted and exhausted, lacking the energy necessary to question whether there is even any truth in the images we carry. So handicapped do we become by the images that are an expression of our negative conditioning that inner wholeness is perceived as a fantasy that bears no relationship to ourselves.

The absurdity and tragedy of our fixation with defending or asserting our images is that our images have little, if anything, to do with the present moment and the resources and possibilities actually available to us in the present. The bulk of our images are rooted in experiences and impressions made upon our consciousness in the past, at times so long ago that those experiences are no longer even consciously carried in our memory. A particularly painful and traumatic experience or a series of them can lead us to construct a negative, limited image that is carried with us throughout our lives.

Ilse was an elderly woman who had inoperable cancer. She was aware that she was dying and her coming to a retreat was going to be one of the last journeys she would make. She told me why she had chosen to spend one of the last weeks of her life in a meditation retreat, and spoke of the burden she carried:

> I'm an old woman, but I'm not ready yet to die. I've made peace with my family but I have not yet made peace with myself, and I don't want to die until I can do that. When I was eight years old, I was raped. My whole life since then I have been afraid of people, terrified they will hurt me. I've been afraid to love almost anyone, because I can't trust anyone. I don't want to die so afraid, feeling so powerless and incapacitated.

The burdens of the past we carry, in conscious and unconscious ways, have the power to pervade and limit every area of our lives. We become debilitated by them and further debilitated by our seeming inability to let go of our burdens. Like a person going on a train journey, we carry our heavy baggage to the station and continue to carry it even when the train has departed, not realizing that we have the freedom to put it down. In our own lives, our lack of awareness and our fear and lack of trust in ourselves doom us to carry the burden of negative images unnecessarily.

The deepening of awareness means that we come to a point in our lives when we are able to drop the burdens we carry. The beginning of letting the past be the past lies in grounding ourselves in the present and acquainting ourselves with the fullness of our being. Connected with the present moment, an openness and awareness begin to emerge that allow us to accept and integrate the past without fear or resistance. Grounding ourselves in our awareness of ourselves in the present, we begin to understand that we need not be victims of the past. Our trust in ourselves deepens as we begin to avail ourselves of the resources of sensitivity and awareness that lie within us right now. This trust empowers us to make new beginnings in each moment in our lives, untainted by the impressions of the past.

Making new beginnings is no easy task for us despite the number of times we are called upon to do so in our lives. Aware of the power of our past impressions, we may feel compelled to attempt to undo the traumas of the past before we can arrive in the present. Certainly, there is validity in gaining a clear and conscious understanding of the impressions and influences of the past. Understanding is the medium of change. Yet to become fixated upon untangling the past is to undertake an endless journey as we encounter layer upon layer of conditioning. Too often in our attempt to untangle the past we assume either the role of the victim who is still fearful of being overwhelmed, or the role of the adversary who sets out to conquer the power of the past. Tied within these roles we become blinded to the possibilities of utilizing our resources in the present to simply see the inherent falseness of the images we carry. Being able to see the false as false: that is all we have to do.

Untying the knots of our conditioning does involve seeing the relationship between ourselves in the past and ourselves in the present. The deepening of our understanding entails being acutely aware of the models, the experiences, and the impressions that have contributed to molding our image of ourselves in the present. It is an awareness without blame, free of blame projected upon ourselves and free of the influence of either the victim or the adversary.

Possibilities of freedom in the present begin to unfold as we inquire into the roles we assume, the life directions we have chosen, and the images we carry at this moment. Are they an expression of freedom or of fear? Are they a manifestation of personal creativity or belief in personal limitation? Are we embarked on a path of fulfilling our potential as women—as whole human beings—or are we treading an anxious path of safety and retreat from our own potential? Do the directions we have chosen in our lives nurture an inner sense of trust and freedom, or are our choices undermining our trust and inner freedom?

They are hard and challenging questions to ask of ourselves. To even begin to ask them, we must in our hearts treasure our freedom and wholeness more than the familiarity of our sanctuaries and roles. No one but ourselves can know the answers and no one but ourselves is qualified to begin to explore the questions. Only we are truly intimate with ourselves and fully know the ways in which we entangle or free ourselves.

Untying the knots of our conditioning, both from the past and in the present, means the willingness to confront our own fear and, possibly, the disapproval of others. It means the willingness to take the risks of venturing beyond the boundaries of the familiar sanctuaries and identities our conditioning defines for us. At times, confronting our conditioning involves grief, anger, and despair. Certainly, it calls for a deep and open awareness. Untangling our knots entails the willingness to experience our aloneness in a positive and creative way and the courage to walk away from the approval and affirmation we too often rely upon.

No image or description of ourselves that is founded upon conditioning can ever be an adequate or total vision of who we actually are. These images and descriptions become a poor and shallow substitute for freedom. The degree of freedom we experience will always be defined by the limits of our images. The experience of repeated conflict, frustration, and resentment within ourselves is a clear message telling us of the lack of wholeness and freedom we miss. Profound discontent speaks to us of unresolved conflict and unfulfilled need: the deepest conflict in our lives is our divorce from our own potential, and our deepest need is the need to be free.

We can react to those conflicts by projecting blame, inwardly or outwardly, or by sinking into passivity. We can react to those conflicts and needs by a constant pursuit of distraction, trying to blanket them with busyness and preoccupation. This, to me, is an expression of immature discontent, the perpetual avoidance of connecting with what we are actually experiencing. There is an experience of mature discontent, when we listen to the sounds and stories of our dissatisfaction and learn from them, when we question the true story and source of our conflicts and question their necessity. This essential openness is the beginning of our capacity to bring about the changes we need and to leave behind the conditioning that undermines us.

Superficially, it would seem that the concepts of spirituality and conditioning are contradictory. But if we explore any path of established spirituality, it is apparent that those paths carry with them specific models, authorities, hierarchies, values, and goals. When we begin to explore a spiritual path, we encounter the belief systems that the tradition upholds and they make a deep impression. In our eagerness to discover the end of conflict, we tend to absorb and adopt the values and models we are exposed to without question. In that adoption, we are actually adopting another subtle, yet very real, form of conditioning.

I do not want to negate the value of tradition nor many of the values it upholds. Along with many others, I have derived great benefit from such tradition. It is, however, important to recognize that there is such a thing as spiritual conditioning and that it has a profound effect upon us. Despite the parallels in our histories and aspirations, each of us is a unique individual. Our pasts, our dreams, our responses, and our inner experience are unique to each of us. There is no standard spiritual map that can be dispensed that will fully address the uniqueness of each of us. Our uniqueness is to be treasured, not to be overcome. We can draw upon the richness of tradition and benefit from the experience and guidance of those who have traveled before us, but in the end, it is only we who can truly understand ourselves, call upon our own resources, and experience and discover our own freedom.

Nurturing our inner capacity to question and inquire is essential in developing a path of spirituality that addresses our uniqueness. A part of that questioning is learning how to honor our doubts. We must not be cowed or intimidated by the weight of authority or tradition if we are to be enriched by them rather than oppressed by them. In the Kalama Sutra, the Buddha encourages both doubt and inquiry in saying,

> Do not believe in something just because it is upheld by tradition or written in scriptures. Do not believe something just because it is spoken by a teacher or upheld through history. Do not believe something because it appears logical or is in concordance with your own views. When you know in yourselves that a teaching is wholesome, blameless, wise, and when put into effect leads to happiness and well-being, that teaching you can believe.

Spiritual conditioning can be no less undermining than any other form of conditioning. Spiritual maturity involves not only untangling the knots of our social and psychological conditioning, but also the knots of our spiritual conditioning. It understands what it means to establish a spiritual home within our own being and our own experience. Certainly, spiritual maturity is not a proficiency in meditation techniques or a sound knowledge of spiritual or religious philosophy. Spiritual maturity is discovering an inner wholeness and freedom born of connecting inwardly with our own resources and our inner capacity to be aware.

A characteristic of an authentic spirituality is that it addresses our own experience and honors our own understanding. This is not to deny or reject the guidance of others, but to acknowledge that a true spiritual path must affirm our trust in ourselves, even to doubt. If we can look for any signpost to affirm the authenticity of a spiritual path, it is that the path we have chosen is in actuality bringing to an end the suffering and conflict in our lives and not sowing the seeds of greater suffering.

Sally joined the devotees of a charismatic teacher. She loved the life and the community of people, who shared aspirations similar to hers. The practice involved surrender of the ego by willingly doing jobs in the ashram that she disliked, bowing, and giving up her attachments to her personal space and inclinations. She felt she was learning a great deal about herself. One day, one of the teacher's assistants came to her and spoke of his loneliness and the isolation imposed upon him by his role. He then suggested that she could further her practice by surrendering herself sexually to him. When she resisted his overtures, she was given to understand that her resistance expressed the identification she had with her body. She was afraid to confide in either the teacher or her companions, doubting the authenticity of her resistance, yet equally doubting the validity of the supposed "teaching" she was receiving. She left the ashram, confused, disillusioned, and in great pain. It was some time before she recovered sufficient confidence in herself to be able to trust a spiritual authority again.

We transfer our own patterns of conditioning to our spiritual lives. Our fear of and obedience to authority, our fears of disapproval and rejection, and our lack of trust in ourselves are not burdens that we leave behind as we begin on a spiritual path. They are carried with us to distort the vision we hold of our spiritual potential and possibilities. We can dress up our habitual patterns of relating and seeing in new disguises and rename them with more attractive labels, yet their renaming does not disguise their continued destructiveness. We will not bypass this conditioning. Our spiritual freedom and maturity rely upon our willingness to question it. It is a freedom that is encouraged by an authentic spiritual path.

As novices in the spiritual life, we do not have a wealth of inner spiritual experience to rely upon, and so naturally we turn to authorities, leaders, and teachers. We look to the authorities we respect for answers to our questions, for guidance, and for inspiration. In the inequality of our roles and our own spiritual uncertainty, we easily adopt the values, models, and beliefs of the tradition without question or regard for their relevance to our own lives. It is all too easy in our spiritual naiveté and inner uncertainty to become locked into the role of being a "follower." Then, being locked into the role of the follower, we equally become locked into the role of the believer. We want to say yes to what we are taught. We want to accept and absorb, because our agreeability is the ticket to belonging, to a spiritual identity. In our eagerness and our earnestness, the spark of inquiry within us remains unkindled. A spiritual path that truly treasures and emphasizes freedom will discourage spiritual consumers who crave a "package deal" by encouraging them to question and inquire, to truly understand the teachings they are integrating.

When we adopt without question the values, beliefs, and goals of others, no matter how worthy they are, it becomes exceedingly difficult to establish a spiritual home within ourselves. Instead, we inhabit the homes of others, where we are truly strangers despite the accord we may share with them. We continue to reside outside ourselves and in doing so, remain estranged from our own freedom and spiritual wholeness.

The conditioning we absorb is not inherent in the teachings or in the authorities we turn to for guidance. The knots of conditioning lie in the *relationships* we form, both with authorities and with belief systems. The quality of relationship that leads us to adopt new forms of conditioning is essentially an unaware relationship. It is a relationship that is characterized by inner uncertainty, fear, and a lack of inner trust.

We perceive authority not just in spiritual teachers, but in the beliefs and values they present. One authority may tell us that everything is out of our control, and in the hands of God, and exhort us to have faith. Another authority will present us with a different version of the path to freedom by explaining that all our conflicts and problems are a result of the past, and that what we have to do is erase the past. Yet another authority will teach that our lack of freedom is rooted in our attachments and identifications, and that a path of asceticism is the way to cut through our attachments.

Blinded by our fascination with authority and our inner uncertainty, we internalize the beliefs, values, paths, and goals of others. Our spiritual vision is conditioned by that absorption.

A major force that encourages that absorption and internalization is our own distorted relationship with authority. Guided by authorities throughout our lives, we transfer our awe of authority to our spirituality, perceiving spiritual authorities as infallible and superhuman. We create models of what spiritual teachers should look like and how they should act and relate. We seek spiritual guides who conform to our own images. During my own pregnancies, I continued to guide retreats; the very fact of my pregnancy confused and puzzled many participants, confronting them with their own models of what a teacher should be. When coming to personal meetings with me, the discomfort of some students was overwhelming to them as they tried to look anywhere but at the great mound of my belly.

Our models of what a spiritual guide is condition our openness, our willingness to learn, and even our capacity to listen. The models we hold tend to be as static and rigid as any other form of conditioning. Our models become blind spots that limit our capacity to perceive the teacher in our relationships, in other people, in ourselves, and in life itself. When we hold our models rigidly, they become unconscious truths that are accepted as reality.

Once, when invited to lead a retreat at a center in the West, I entered the meditation room to discover that the place designated for me to sit was occupied by an Eastern monk who had been staying at the center for some time. His rules of conduct decreed that he had to sit on a seat higher than laypeople, and certainly higher than women, despite the fact that I was actually the retreat leader. Deciding that his rules were not my rules, I went to sit on the podium beside him. I sensed his horror at my seeming lack of suitable respect for him as he opened his eyes and saw me sitting beside him. He then began to slowly but surely edge away from me until he was teetering on the edge of the podium. The next day when I came into the meditation room, we repeated the same ritual, he in my place, I sitting beside him, and again there was a shuffle to separate himself from me. When he took his grievances to the staff at the center and they explained that as retreat leader I was meant to sit at the front of the hall, he felt unable to live with the dishonor of sitting beside a woman and left the center.

Our spiritual paths are conditioned by the models that we carry, and equally by the value systems we create and absorb. Asceticism, in varying degrees, is an integral and historical aspect of both Eastern and Western spiritual value systems. A dualism is created between the goals of spirituality—enlightenment, oneness, and freedom—and the actualities of who and where we are in our lives. The path to those goals is frequently interpreted as being a path of overcoming, transcending, and renouncing the actualities of ourselves that seem to hinder the attainment of our goals. It is an interpretation that is expressed in varying forms of self-punishment and inner brutality.

Positive values are attributed to enlightenment and oneness, whereas negative values are attributed to whatever is perceived as an obstacle to our goals, be it our sexuality, our body, or our emotions. Our spiritual work is then seen as negating the negative. Absorbing these values, we perceive the path of spirituality essentially as being a path that entails great suffering and misery. In fact, the degree of suffering we experience is even equated with the degree of depth we are gaining in our spiritual unfoldment. It is felt that the more miserable we are, the deeper we are going. In my own participation in intensive meditation, I remember feeling a sense of envy toward those who would weep or collapse in the meditation room, feeling that they must be going really deep and coming to grips with their impurities.

It is a misinterpretation of spirituality and depth in spiritual development to perceive the spiritual life as a life of misery and joylessness. There is pain and grief in our deepening awareness of the knots that limit us. There is great joy in that awareness, too, knowing that our awareness is liberating. There is great joy in connecting with the inner resources that empower us to transform and understand without brutality or self-punishment.

Spiritual values are absorbed from others and created within. We must be willing to understand those values clearly in the context of our own experience, so that they do not become yet another knot that confuses and limits us. Mystics in all traditions have advocated the need for renunciation if we are to be free. We perceive the truth in this and begin to practice renunciation without necessarily questioning what quality of renunciation is called for and what it is we need to renounce to discover our own freedom. In our application of renunciation, we might not go to the extreme of burning our homes and possessions, yet we might find ourselves assuming conscious and unconscious stances of aversion toward our connections and bonds with life and other people.

It is a short step from aversion to rejection. In the distortion of our perception of the value of renunciation, we may perceive the world only in the light of being empty, something to get out of. We may perceive our relationships only in the light of attachment, ties to be rejected. We may perceive our bodies and sexuality only as impure, to be transcended. We learn to guard our senses against the invasion of temptation. In this distortion of renunciation, we reject physical and emotional experience, even beauty and love, and exalt the spiritual, which is perceived as being above such worldly experience.

We create and absorb value systems without questioning whether those values are intrinsically truthful. We may not even question whether the value systems we hold are furthering our spiritual growth or inhibiting it. If we do begin to question, we see that there is nothing inherently binding in the world or in our connections with it. There is nothing intrinsically impure in our bodies, in our sexuality, or in our joy at watching the sun setting. True renunciation is born of love and compassion, not of aversion and rejection. Renunciation is not a severance or denial, but a letting go of any value or projection that inhibits freedom.

Our misinterpretation of renunciation and nonattachment is further exaggerated to distort our belief in what a spiritual mode of life is. A spiritual life becomes defined as a withdrawal from the world, a separating of ourselves from other people. We feel we further our spirituality only when we close our eyes and turn inward. We glamorize the monastic life as being the truest and profoundest expression of spirituality. Needless to say, this glamorization decrees that a family life or a life that is lived amid worldly connections and activity is spiritually inferior. The conclusions we draw prevent us from seeing that there is nothing inherently spiritual about logging time on a meditation cushion or kneeling in prayer. We can meditate and be truly aware and sensitive. We can equally go through the motions and compile our shopping lists or dwell on our ill will toward another.

When our spirituality becomes a path of rejection or a path that is based upon conditioned values, our spirituality essentially moves from our hearts to our minds. Our values determine that our meditation and contemplation become judges of what we experience rather than appreciation of what unfolds in each moment and within ourselves. We evaluate, compare, and judge our experience in the moment on the basis of our conditioned values, rather than maintaining a state of openness in which we are capable of learning from the moment and from ourselves.

The reality of our experience as human beings is that we yearn for bonding and communion with others. Sociologists and psychologists confirm that such bonding and communion are integral to our growth and to our trust in ourselves. Holding distorted values of attachment, we judge these yearnings and decree them to be signs of our spiritual weakness. We learn to see our yearnings for bonding as problems to get over, and feel we must become stronger, less vulnerable, less needy. Lost in our conditioning, we use our values to invalidate our responses and our trust in ourselves.

When spiritual development is distorted by spiritual conditioning, spiritual success is equated with the power to invalidate ourselves. Selflessness is awarded the value of being the ultimate spiritual goal. Perceived through the filters of distorted values, selflessness is equated with self-negation and self-denial. We invalidate ourselves by doubting and denying our own responses, we invalidate ourselves by dismissing our intuitions as sentimental, and we invalidate ourselves by striving for spiritual goals that denigrate our own being.

Selflessness is not the negation of self-trust or self-respect. We need to trust and respect ourselves to nurture our spiritual integrity and wholeness. The destructive forces of greed, aggression, and hatred will not be erased by self-punishment. They will be ended by deeply understanding their destructiveness to our own well-being and the well-being of our world. Selfishness is truly an absence of the capacity to honor and respect our own dignity and spirit and the spirit of our world. Selflessness is the honoring and cherishing of our mutual interconnectedness, well-being, and dignity. It is not a goal to be achieved through rejection or denial, but is realized through a deep inner connection with our own spirituality that is not distorted by conditioned values.

It is not enough to blame spiritual authorities or traditions for the spiritual conditioning we accumulate. We perpetuate that conditioning and inner invalidation through carrying with us a history of conditioning that leads us to doubt and negate ourselves. It is a history that has conditioned us to listen outwardly more fully than we are able to listen inwardly. Even when we begin to listen inwardly, our listening is compromised by the filters of conditioning that lead us to disbelieve the truths we hear. To continue to blame men, tradition, or institutions for denying our spirituality is symptomatic of our unreadiness to be alone and trust in our own spiritual awakening. For surely, the reverse side of accusation is justification and a subtle seeking of approbation. The truths that will free us of conditioning lie within our own awareness and our hearing of them is facilitated by trusting in ourselves.

We need to learn how to question in a creative way and how to nurture our vision of our spiritual potential by clearly connecting with our inner resources of awareness. Learning how to listen openly, with wise discrimination, we can benefit from the heritage and richness of spiritual tradition. Trusting in our own experience and understanding, we can listen inwardly and discard values that contradict our own understanding or undermine our inner freedom.

We learn from our own histories, and we learn from the present moment. Untying the knots of our conditioning means truly understanding that there is nothing more significant in life than abiding in deep inner wholeness and freedom. The wholeness and freedom we discover within ourselves are the vehicle for the love, sensitivity, and compassion we give to our world.

## *Meditation on Untying the Knots* ...

We carry within us knots of distorted beliefs that hinder us in our quest for freedom and wholeness. Our knots, which are rooted in the past, are created through undermining experiences and conditioning. Untangling those knots is not a question of erasing or denying the past: our knots are untangled through dissolving our belief in them as being true descriptions of who we are. Awareness and understanding are the tools for seeing clearly. All that we need for transformation lies within ourselves in this moment we are experiencing.

Let yourself settle into a posture that is comfortable. Harmonizing your attention with your breath, release any tension or holding you are experiencing in your body or mind. Feel the stillness of your body, and relax into that stillness. Feel the rhythm and movement of your breath and the space in between your breaths. Feel the stillness and receptivity of yourself in that space between each out and in breath. Let yourself merge into that stillness, feeling your breath as just a whisper in the stillness.

Bring your attention just to listening, neither looking for sound nor labeling any sound that comes to you. Just be receptive to sounds arising and passing and to the silence between sounds. Let yourself merge into the silence of receptivity, being present with just listening. Allow yourself to be still inwardly, appreciating the richness and sensitivity of receptivity. Just settle into the moment, appreciating the silence and spaciousness within yourself and the silence and spaciousness that embrace you.

Expand your awareness to let it enfold the thoughts and feelings that are arising and passing within you, just being present without dwelling or judgment, being present with receptivity. Be aware of how those thoughts and feelings arise and pass in stillness, aware of the stillness between the thoughts, and aware of the stillness that holds the thoughts, the stillness that is without judgment or prejudice.

In that stillness, reflect for a moment on the knots that you feel bind you. They may be knots of self-denial, beliefs in powerlessness, fears of aloneness, or beliefs in incompleteness. They may be knots of resentment, of jealousy, or of mistrust. Let the stillness within embrace your reflection, free from denial and judgment. Extend warmth and generosity to yourself, filling yourself with sensitivity and openness.

In that stillness, visualize an ocean, the constant movement of its waves touching the shore and receding. See the swell and fall of the powerful waves, see the crests of the waves as they break, see the playfulness of the waves as they touch the shore in ripples, and see the foam upon the water. See how the movements and changes within yourself are so much like the movements within the ocean. Some of the knots we carry are powerful: they submerge everything before them. Some of the knots we carry are less formed: like currents in the water, they pull and push us in our lives. Some of the knots we carry are like the gentle waves that touch the shore, and some of the knots we carry are like the foam upon the water.

At times, the waves are stormy and powerful; equally, the water can be a still pool that reflects everything within it. The crests, the swells, and the foam: all are born of the same water. The water is not for or against the variety of waves that play upon it: it makes no judgment but simply embraces. Let yourself be still in the ocean, the vastness of your own awareness. Let yourself embrace the variety of waves that play upon it. Let the vastness of your own awareness reflect clearly the ripples and crests that unfold. Let yourself open to the variety of movements that touch you, knowing that you need not be swept away by any of those movements.

The knots within us arise, at times with great power. We can be still and present; we can be open and expansive. We can be one with that stillness and vastness, and embrace the waves within just as the ocean embraces its own waves. In that stillness, release the knots. In knowing your oneness with the vastness of your awareness, the knots release and untangle themselves. Allow yourself to merge into that oneness, with gentleness, with openness, and with love.

# Chapter 5
## *Power*

W E NEED TO UNDERSTAND deeply the place of power in our
lives, what it means to us now and what it can mean to us.
Every hierarchy, structure, and system that evolves holds within it the element of power. It is a central and unavoidable issue in our lives, which by
their very nature are tied to structures and systems.

Apart from the political, social, and religious structures we willingly or
unwillingly participate in or are subjected to, our survival —as the human
race and as individuals—entails participating in relationships with nature
and with one another that are characterized by need and dependency. As
infants, we depend upon others for our nurturing; throughout our lives, we
depend upon nature for our sustenance. Our physical, emotional, and psychological well-being is founded upon our needs being responded to by
forces and people who hold the power to respond to or to deny the needs
we express.

Relationship is never one-sided: the well-being of our children, our
planet, and the people we interact with depend inevitably upon our own
responses and sustenance. Mutual dependency is the basis of survival and
relationship, and power is a basic ingredient of dependency. Nature's first law
is the law of the interconnectedness, the interdependence of all life. It is an
expression not of weakness but of wisdom both to acknowledge this primary law of nature and to recognize that the qualities of mutual need and
dependency are fundamental principles of relationship and survival. It is an
acknowledgment that is essential if we are to utilize our own power and
relate to the power of others creatively, rather than destructively.

We invest the quality of power with a variety of associations, meanings,
and connotations. Some perceive power as a force and as a possession that
is desirable, exciting, and attractive. Others see it as frightening and anxiety-

provoking, a force to be avoided. Inevitably, we perceive the presence, pressure, and influence of power all around us and within ourselves.

The evolution of our technology ensures that we hold the power to manipulate and influence nature in ways that can be either creative or destructive. Through the power that our knowledge has provided us with, we can increase the abundance of our harvests to relieve suffering. Equally, we hold the power to devastate the ecology of our planet, to harvest only untold suffering and deprivation. George Wald remarks, "It is our culture alone among the cultures of the Earth that has brought the technology of killing and destruction much further than any culture on the Earth ever dreamed of doing before."[1] We mindlessly manipulate nature to fulfill our needs and desires, failing to appreciate that the devastation we wreak upon nature has, in turn, the power to threaten the quality of our lives and our very survival itself. By the misuse of our power—by seeing it as a weapon rather than a gift—and by our dismissal of Nature's law of interconnectedness, we will bequeath to future generations a planet that is irreversibly damaged.

Objects, authorities, models, parents, and situations we encounter can exert a power over us that is considerable and, at times, frightening. In the face of negative feedback from others, we can find ourselves doubting our roles, directions, and achievements and revert to the child within, who needs approval and affirmation above all else, including inner respect.

At the end of her first year at medical school, Joan found herself at the top of her class. Her initial elation at her success was soon tempered when she found herself isolated by the resentment and envy of some of her classmates. The results of her academic achievement served to cast her in the role of social leper. She experienced the rejection and dismissal of her peers as a more powerful force than her own self-esteem. The following year, Joan expressed her overwhelming need for affirmation by ensuring that her grades were only average.

We experience the immense power of our own thoughts, feelings, memories, images, and desires as they mold our consciousness, our ways of seeing ourselves and the world. We feel ourselves at times to be victims of our minds and our past, pushed without choice from one extreme of feeling to another. We feel we are ensnared by our memories and desires as they propel us to act and relate in ways that undermine our own well-being and our relationships. More positively, we can feel the effects of our own power in relation to people, objects, and circumstances, expanding our sense of capability, possibility, and effectiveness. Equally, we feel the effects of our misuse of power when it causes a corresponding sense of inadequacy and ineffectiveness within.

Our world resonates with power, recoils from its misuse, and is enriched by its skillful application. We have felt the pain and withdrawal that we have known at the hands of those who have exerted a destructive power over us, whether intentional or unintentional. We have felt, too, the joy and nurturing at the hands of those who have given freely of their creative and liberating power.

We must recognize that we all have power. We must understand its sources, its potential, and its effects, so that we can draw upon the creative wealth of power rather than be destroyed by it. We must learn to question the messages of our culture, which insist that power lies only outside ourselves, in authorities and hierarchical structures, or we will learn to disbelieve in our own power and suffer a paralysis of personal effectiveness.

Power centers are created through thought and belief, based upon fear or upon inner strength. The center for our thoughts and beliefs lies within ourselves: therefore, we can either grant or withhold power. It is proclaimed by the Catholic Church that women may not serve communion; it is proclaimed by elders in Theravadan Buddhism that women may not assume the role of a fully ordained *bhikkhuni*. Asking permission to serve communion, women instead are invited to serve at church bazaars; asking permission for full ordination, women are invited to explore their inner potential for service and humility.

These proclamations are effective only as long as power is given to authorities to make these proclamations. Without collaboration, these proclamations fall within a vacuum. We are dispossessed of our own power and effectiveness only as long as we are possessed by our own belief that the source of power lies in centers and structures outside ourselves.

Power is energy, energy that can influence, change, destroy, or transform. Power is energy that has the potential to condition our behavior and our vision of ourselves. Power is also an inner energy that can be called upon to effect change in our environment or in ourselves. It is an energy that permeates our world, our social structures, and our own being. In a patriarchal culture, power is equated with the capacity to have power over something: it is the capacity to control, to alter, to manipulate, or to influence the world. This capacity to control builds a sense of strength, an illusion of invincibility. Cloaking ourselves in power, we can manipulate and control our world while protecting ourselves from the effects of our power.

The ability to control other people, circumstances, or oneself creates an inflated self-image, an image that in our culture is generally equated with success, no matter how questionable that power or control may be. Success is seen as a personal accolade, to be achieved regardless of the cost of its achievement. The rules defining success, which depend on control and mastery, have come to shape work itself and the work process. Work then becomes a function of success rather than success being a by-product of work. The prospect of success and its price is seen by many women to be disturbing if not frightening.

Gillian excelled at business school and was offered employment in a prestigious management company upon graduation. She began her job at the same time as two other employees, and the competition for promotion was intense from the beginning. Moving up the ladder of success demanded her absolute dedication, which initially she gave, both because she wanted to prove herself and because of the enjoyment she derived from her work. After a year on the job, she began to suffer anxiety attacks and severe headaches, and was advised by her doctor to relax and enjoy life. She felt herself unable to heed his advice, for to do so would clearly involve sacrificing the success she desired. Hiding her personal difficulties, she managed after another year to achieve the executive status she was pursuing, only to discover the drastic price she had paid. She had professional relationships fraught with ambition and rivalry, yet was bereft of the type of meaningful relationships that might have offered her communication and support. She had created an image of an independent, self-contained professional, but this very image was perceived as threatening and alienating to many of the acquaintances she made. She had success but also deep feelings of loneliness and inadequacy. The shallowness and tension of her inner and outer life helped her to understand that achievement and fulfillment were very different experiences.

We might well question whether any of our social structures are free from the influence of the distorted use of power, which equates control and mastery with success. Success in parent–child relationships and in adult relationships is too frequently measured by the capacity to control another, to call forth an unquestioning obedience and loyalty. The price of control is high. In developing power or mastery over anything, we set ourselves against that which we wish to control: we set ourselves against people, against events, against nature, or even against our own nature.

With the desire for mastery comes a distancing from that which we seek to control. The distance is essential to create and preserve: it serves to prevent us from being overwhelmed by the power of others and to protect ourselves from fear. We desire to master all that we have learned to despise and that we feel threatened by; and whether the sources of our fear are inward or outward, control and distance are the tools we use to subdue our fear and assert our power. When the sources of our fear lie outside ourselves, debasement and humiliation become the vehicles through which we are able to assert our mastery and control. Fear, resentment, anger, and the projection of anger onto a scapegoat are the processes through which destructive power is created. Colonizers, victors in war, racists, and chauvinists all use the tools of debasement and humiliation to protect themselves from fear and to assert their mastery.

Life can seem like one long, intense struggle for supremacy. We are in the realm of win or lose; winning becomes a measure and a test of our personal worth, and competition is the necessary field of activity. To participate in the game, we must be schooled in the necessary skills involved in winning, skills that are contrary to a cooperative relationship with life that treasures well-being and respects interconnectedness. We must learn to pursue our goals single-mindedly while ignoring the repercussions of our pursuit upon others. We must learn to cultivate ambition and agency without regard for the consequences; we must learn to deny anything that hampers our pursuit.

A woman's conditioning does not lend itself to the pursuit of success on these terms. The price she pays in participating in power-dominated structures and systems that glorify success is, all too frequently, the rejection of her own inner voice that calls for cooperation and mutuality and its replacement by the stridency of ambition and competitiveness. Frequently, women feel they are held back by their conditioning and psychological makeup: they fail to appreciate the invaluable contribution that their disposition and yearning for interconnectedness can offer to the dissolution and transformation of destructive systems that are based on the notion of mastery over others. Superficially, men appear to benefit from the systems that prevail in our society, but in the end, we all suffer.

Women desiring to pursue a career experience themselves as being caught in an either/or situation. Either they cultivate a life that is focused upon developing a deep sense of relatedness with others, responding to their intuitive desire for connectedness, or they relinquish this in order to succeed in a career that may be lacking in the relatedness they seek. Too often, these are seen as opposing choices rather than mutually enhancing options. Yet they are opposing choices only so long as they are seen in the context of accepted social and professional structures. Increasingly, as women begin to assert their capabilities and effectiveness in every structure within our culture, they must also begin to trust in their capacity to transform those structures. Systems and structures are created to serve us: we are not created to serve them. They exist as rigid power structures, absolved from change, only as long as we collude in giving power to them.

Sheila was a successful lawyer specializing in mental health rights. She was hired to join a team of lawyers involved with a major health institution. A clear hierarchy existed, with the director of the team distributing the workload on which each member worked independently. Sheila found herself with many cases to deal with and, despite her initial deep concern for the welfare of the individuals she was defending, she found herself beginning to reduce them to statistics, "cases" that she either won or lost. One day, she realized that she was more concerned with paperwork than with people, that what to her had become "cases" were people's lives and futures. She also realized that the depersonalization that had become the norm was a result of her attitudes and the attitudes of her co-workers, not a by-product of the work itself. Sheila had sufficient trust in her insight and concern for her clients to call a meeting of her co-workers and express her apprehensions about reducing people's lives to "cases." After much discussion, she discovered that the apprehensions she experienced were shared by her co-workers, and they shared together valid ways to bring about a change in their attitudes. Team meetings and personal contact with their clients rather than just with clients' social workers, among other changes, brought a greater sense of personal connection, heart, and meaningfulness to their work.

It is only a matter of degree to move from seeing life as competition to seeing life as a battle. The need to win becomes the need to conquer, and the need for power over others and the environment expresses itself in racism, sexism, war, genocide, and the rape of Nature. The underlying threads of the misuse of power run through all patterns of destruction. If we measure our work and the quality of our lives by our capacity to control and to win, then we must win at any cost, for to lose is to be a failure. It is failure itself that brings us face-to-face with our vulnerability and our fear.

Vulnerability and openness are misunderstood and confused with weakness, sentimentality, and powerlessness. We are only compelled to win, to be invincible, and to exert power over others only as long as we fear our own vulnerability. We appear to avoid being overwhelmed by fear as long as we are winning, but our gains are fragile and we must continue to protect them through mastery and distancing if we are not to fall into the pit of failure. Whether we are seen to be winning or losing, the effects are pain, suffering, and alienation, inflicted on ourselves and others.

The evolvement of the structures and systems that dominate Western and much of Eastern society tell the story of the glorification of mastery, control, and exerting power over our environment: the ending of the story is not a happy one. Patriarchy dominates our cultural structures and systems, investing them with power, building into them the authority to dictate value systems and guidelines for measuring personal worth. Women have been divested of power and effectiveness in the evolvement of our social structures, and learn to see themselves as powerless and ineffective.

The fundamentals of human life—giving birth, healing and dying—were traditionally the territory of women and in the care of women. Historically, these fundamental principles of living were celebrated by women through ritual. Ritual gave meaning to the events of birth, menstruation, healing, and death; ritual also bonded the women together, and that bonding gave power. It was a power both respected and feared by male-dominated structures. On the one hand, everyone, without exception, was dependent upon the power that women had over giving birth and healing, and so they respected it. On the other hand, it was women alone who held the keys to the mysteries of giving life and healing sickness, and their power was feared by the men, who were excluded from it. As the power of male-dominated structures evolved, women were dispossessed of their power over the fundamentals of living. With their eviction from their traditional territory, women were also deprived of the bonding that they strengthened through ritual.

Birth was a time of celebration, of women joining together to support one another and rejoice in the power of their own bodies and the gift of life. Skilled midwives, attuned to the rhythms of their own bodies, could listen to and respond to the messages of the expectant mother. That momentous occasion, giving birth, is now all too frequently reduced to a time of anxiety and fear. Too often drugged, stripped of dignity, and lying in a posture of passivity—a spectator divorced from the power and forces of her own body—a woman has her child delivered for her in the sterility of a managed labor. We see an epidemic of cesarean deliveries as doctors endeavor to control the entire birth process. The problem of a mother finding difficulty in bonding with her newborn child is only an extension of the alienation inflicted upon her in the birth process.

In both of my own pregnancies, when I stated my intention to deliver my children at home naturally, I met with a wall of opposition. Passed along the hierarchy of birth attendants, from nurse to midwife, both women, I at last arrived at the pinnacle of the hierarchy, a male consultant, who could only admonish me about the foolishness of my decision, my lack of care for my child, and my ignorance about my body and giving birth, admonishments given despite the fact that my pregnancies were healthy and free of complications. At a time of great vulnerability, when the quality we need most is inner trust, the lack of support from the medical profession sows the seeds of doubt within us. The births of my children at home, supported by friends and caring midwives, have been among the most profound and joyful experiences of my life.

Our ancestors learned to draw upon the wealth of nature to heal; these healing women, attuned to the inner and outer rhythms of life, concerned themselves with healing the whole person. Victimized for their skills, labeled formerly as witches, latterly as cranks, they were and are divested of their healing power through the formation of power systems governed by male-dominated structures. From the fourteenth through the seventeenth century, millions of women were indiscriminately murdered as witches in Europe and the United States. These women were depicted as witches for their service to peasant communities as healers and midwives. The wise women frightened not only the medical establishment, but also the entire feudal system through their network of underground communication and their function as political matrices in the peasant communities.[2] The witch-hunter manual states, "No one does more harm to the Catholic faith than midwives."[3]

Women also brought an aura of grace to dying. By bonding together they aided and supported the dying process in order to lend dignity and meaning to the life–death transition. Grief was expressed through ritual, and through that expression, healing could begin. Now even the process of dying is governed by the dictates of power structures that lie outside ourselves and determine how and even when death should occur. Hidden behind isolated hospital screens, what other associations can death assume but fear and anxiety? Overpowered by the social expectations to be strong and brave, how difficult it is to heal our grief and loss. Being able to embrace death as part of our living experience is an integral part of being able to embrace life.

Shelley waited with her family while her son underwent emergency surgery for a brain tumor. The surgeon entered and beckoned her father aside. They approached her, saying, "You must be strong. Jacob has died." Her cry of grief was quelled with a tranquilizer. She attended his funeral dry-eyed, numbed by sedatives, and was admired by all for her courage and strength. She also withdrew from her other children, feeling unable to give them the love and affection they needed. Years later, she spoke of the tremendous need she had experienced just to cry and to be held, and her inability to experience and integrate her grief because of the expectations she perceived from others that she must be a pillar of strength.

The fear of the bonding power that women exhibited through their rituals, as well as their individual powers of healing and creating life, led to the formation of power structures that sought to divest women of power. We can only hold in ridicule the label "progress" that this divestment has assumed. We can only celebrate the reclaiming of power by women now taking place in our culture as they discard their own belief in the power structures that attempt to dominate them.

The other half of winning is losing: the companion of the master is the victim. When we believe in power as being only an external force, we find ourselves repeatedly influenced and conditioned by the power of other people or circumstances. At times, the role of the victim is habitually assumed because we carry within our memories scars caused by being overpowered, scars inflicted by the experience of having distorted or perverse power exerted over us. If we adopt the role of the powerless, we actually become powerless.

The experience of being exploited, undermined, or abused inflicts a pain severe enough to make us withdraw from life, creating barriers and defenses to protect ourselves from further pain, thus isolating us still further. Withdrawal reinforces the power that people, situations, and authorities have over us, which, in turn, reinforces our fear of others and reduces us to a state of powerlessness. The belief in our powerlessness conditions our response to life. We go through life afraid: afraid of people, of authority, of change, of our capacity to be hurt, and of our own powerlessness. We are then easily overwhelmed and overcome: we are open to exploitation and abuse.

Powerlessness means paralysis, being incapable of acting outside our relationship to fear. Powerlessness means suppression of thought, feelings, and action, because to express any of these means confronting our fear of power. Powerlessness makes us passive, so that we are acted upon rather than acting. We feel directionless, because the assertion of direction means asserting our own power. As a result of these feelings, we come to feel worthless, unable to contribute anything meaningful to anyone, and equally unable to bring forth change within ourselves. We become angry and resentful toward those perceived as being more powerful than ourselves and, more lethally, toward ourselves, debilitating ourselves still further by self-negation and self-judgment.

When Marilyn and Steve married, both were well established in their respective careers of photographer and writer. When Marilyn became pregnant with their first child, they agreed that the care of the child and their household would be shared and that a short time after the birth Marilyn would return to work, both of their work schedules being flexible enough to allow the sharing of child care. After the birth occurred, Marilyn's return to work was gradually postponed. Steve's schedule did not seem so flexible after all, and the baby seemed to respond to Marilyn better. Soon their days settled into a predictable routine, with Marilyn getting up with the baby in the morning and preparing breakfast for them all. She was already up, so why not? Steve then retreated into his study to work, Marilyn looked after the house and the baby, and Steve praised her for the fine job she was doing when he checked to see if lunch was ready. When she broached the subject of returning to work, Steve very rationally pointed out that surely the work she was doing now was more important than her career. With the loss of her own identity outside the family structure, Marilyn increasingly found herself asking Steve's permission to make even small adjustments in their routine: permission grudgingly given when it did not upset his own schedule unduly. As she became increasingly resentful and volatile, he found it increasingly difficult to understand what she really wanted. She was able to communicate the sources of her resentment and easily able to pinpoint Steve's lack of contribution to their life, but she could not break out of her own paralysis of direction. Only when her emotional crisis became intense was she able to see that what she was seeking from Steve was permission to assert her own power: something he was incapable of granting. Believing in our own powerlessness, we seek protection and safety, only to find ourselves resenting both the source of our protection and our need of it. We feel powerless to free ourselves of either. Like a moth incinerating itself upon the light it craves, we undermine ourselves through our belief in our own powerlessness.

A belief in powerlessness leads us to look for identities that promise safety and roles that are rooted in defensiveness. We look outwards for approval and affirmation, using feedback from the world, whether from established power centers or individuals, to define our sense of worth. Inevitably, this means hyperbolic swings in our sense of self, dependent as we are on the nature of the feedback. Like leaves blown in the wind, we are blown whichever way the wind blows. Instead of living according to what we feel to be true, we live according to what seems to be safe. Instead of trusting in ourselves and in our own worth, we create a foundation for being that is established outside ourselves.

We may believe in powerlessness, but the very resentment and anger it generates illustrates that we cannot accept it. We seek subtler ways of controlling, using our anger and our bitterness to manipulate individuals. We may be reduced to using our sexuality as a weapon, using our feminine wiles to control another person. We may use our very helplessness, our inability to cope, to force another person into the role of protector or to achieve the fulfillment of our needs and desires. In exhibiting ourselves as sex objects or victims, we may attain the immediate ends we desire, but in doing so severely erode our feelings of self-worth and perpetuate the contempt in which we hold ourselves. Our sense of well-being can survive rejection and disapproval from others: it cannot survive self-negation.

We may find ourselves turning to spirituality, looking for the surcease of pain and suffering. Spirituality is essentially concerned with inner freedom and the articulation of that freedom in every area of our lives. The path of spirituality is one of developing a refined awareness that nurtures our own inner wisdom and resources. This inner attunement brings union; integration among our physical, emotional, and psychological selves; and, simultaneously, oneness between our inner life and the life forces by which we are surrounded. Inner wisdom is a vision that transcends the conceptual, rational mind. It cannot be defined, only experienced. We cannot gain it, but only be touched by it. It cannot be earned: we can only open ourselves to it through trusting in the voice of the mystic within. We must hold our aim of freedom close to our hearts, so that we are not distracted by systems, structures, power centers, or authorities that invalidate our inner trust.

The feminine mystic must be willing to set aside a need for approval and sanction from established religion, for it will be reluctantly given. The power centers of patriarchal-dominated structures rest upon the subjugation of the female for the continuation of their power. The scriptures of world religions differ in their beliefs concerning the spiritual life, but concur in their belief about the role of women in it: "A woman must never be free of subjugation" (The Hindu Code of Manu V); "I thank thee, O Lord, that thou hast not created me a woman'" (a daily Orthodox Jewish prayer); "Wives, submit yourselves unto your husbands . . . for the husband is the head of the wife, even as Christ is head of the church" (Ephesians 5:23–24); and "All nuns, no matter how senior, must bow down to all monks, no matter how junior" (Buddhist rules of conduct).

The path of spirituality and the search for freedom are aspirations that seek a form for development and expression. Self-discovery is the basis of developing our spiritual potential and inner wisdom, and the form it takes encompasses a variety of techniques drawn from both Eastern and Western disciplines. Prayer, visualization, and meditation are all practical methods of self-exploration that stress developing inner awareness. Common to any spiritual practice directed toward inner freedom is the idea that it is a direct means of empowering ourselves. Implicit in self-discovery is the notion of learning to trust ourselves, our inner responses, our own awareness, and our experience, and discarding all value systems and types of conditioning that distort or undermine our freedom.

To be with ourselves in meditation, either alone or in the company of others, is a symbol of reclaiming power and utilizing the power of our inner resources of attention and sensitivity to nurture our freedom. That action is the turning away from models and images of who we "should" be and the direction of our energy towards the discovery of who we actually are. Authority over our own lives and being is established inwardly, in inner wisdom, enabling us to direct our lives and our development from a place of deep inner conviction and power. The techniques we choose to employ to address our different needs and inclinations are not as significant as reclaiming our power to develop them in a way that will bring us to inner wholeness.

In the process of self-discovery, we cannot afford to ignore power structures that influence our lives, but neither can we afford to ignore the ways in which we validate destructive power structures through our own distorted relationships to them. We must discover inner sources of creative power and learn to trust in them, thus ending our inclination to give our power over to anyone or anything.

> And you who think to seek for me—
> Know that your seeking and yearning will avail you not
> Unless you know the Mystery:
> That if that which you seek you find not within you,
> You shall never find it without.
> For behold: I have been with you from the beginning,
> And I am that which is attained at the end of desire.[4]

This discovery entails calling upon our own resources of energy, the perseverance to sustain inner exploration and the dedication needed to nurture the inner work necessary to bring wholeness and integration inwardly. If we treasure freedom, we must equally treasure the path to it, discard passivity, and be willing to undertake the journey of self-discovery with commitment and discernment. Acknowledging that our spiritual journey calls for a practical form and expression does not imply that we necessarily need experts to define our journey for us, but neither does it deny that we can benefit deeply from both the practical and mystical experience of others. We can only be enriched by the experience of others if it encourages us to develop our own inner wisdom, to learn from our own experience, and to nurture inner trust. We will be undermined by the guidance of others if it encourages us to blindly adopt value systems that contradict our own wisdom and experience, or to relinquish power by submitting or conforming to sanctioned structures and systems that do not have our freedom at heart. There is little spiritual value in becoming a follower, in adopting the uniform, codes, and rituals of an established spiritual system: we become no more than a safe prisoner of the system we adopt.

There are a variety of forms and expressions of spiritual practice available that enhance awareness, insight, and sensitivity without the sacrifice of inner trust or power. In the path of self-discovery, the path of nurturing the mystic within, the tools we need for awakening lie within us. In the very act of consciously directing our awareness to the present moment, whether we focus upon the breath, the body, feelings, thought processes, or silence, we consciously reclaim power, a power that is creative and transforming. In that conscious focusing, there develops both clarity of attention and inner sensitivity. Essentially, we tune in to what is taking place within the moment, without resistance, rejection, or preoccupation. Awareness is not born but rediscovered, an awareness that is sensitive and open enough to embrace with gentleness the whole tapestry of our being and our fundamental connectedness with all life.

Within this awareness and receptivity, free of control or suppression, the mystic within emerges in a way that integrates every aspect of our being. In the simplicity of awareness that shines as we no longer involve ourselves in control and rejection, we connect more deeply with the patterns of relationship within that are destructive and our own resources that are creative and nurturing. In this clarity of attention, we discover within ourselves sources of both creative and destructive power, power that is undermining as well as power that is transforming. We see clearly that the patterns of relationship that create pain in our outer lives are not separate from the patterns of relationship with ourselves. We see that the patterns of power that we have developed in our lives are transferred to our spiritual paths and influence their development and our vision of ourselves.

If our fear of aloneness has driven us to seek sanctuary in relationship, predictable roles, or conventional attitudes, we may find ourselves eagerly seeking to attach our spiritual umbilical cords to a new protector: a guru, a tradition, or a belief system. Our fear of disapproval and abandonment will guarantee our spiritual obedience and, too frequently, our conformity. The transference of dependency and insecurity to our spiritual paths will stifle our spiritual creativity and freedom, perpetuating the suffocation we seek to escape from.

Anna became a nun with the intention of taking some time out to discover who she really was. She found herself resisting the limitations of the codes of conduct dispensed to the women in the monastery. She felt that her observance of the spoken and unspoken rules for women in the center served to suppress her understanding of herself, instead of deepening that understanding. She struggled for a time to be a good nun, but the escalation of tension she experienced impelled her to question her motivations in desiring to be a good nun. She had been told by one of the Eastern nuns when she entered the monastery, "The woman who makes a good nun is a good daughter," and she began to understand the ways in which she was simply repeating her own distorted relationships with power and authority against a different background and within a different role. That insight enabled her to see that understanding her own relationship to power and authority was not separate from understanding who she really was.

If we see life as a battleground that requires mastery and control over events and people, we will equally believe in the need to master and control ourselves. The battle becomes an inner battle in which we war against ourselves. The battle lines are drawn as particular qualities are lined up on the side of positive value: love, compassion, and wisdom; also detachment, rationality, and renunciation, to name only a few. Hostile to these are the qualities invested with negative value, such as anger, confusion, and dullness, as well as fear, emotion, and, too often, our bodies.

Judgment, both inner and outer, becomes the arbiter of value—and the war is on. Our judgments are rooted in our thoughts, which are conditioned by our past. The negative elements appear to have the power to threaten and overwhelm the positive elements. God, truth, morality, or simply social values can be perceived as the overseer of the battle. There is a constant feeling of being invaded, but we are being invaded by ourselves. The cry of

*Why can't I overcome my past? My negativity? My selfishness? My anger?* is the call of despair of the spiritual warrior.

If we choose meditation as the context for our inner journey and uphold this elaborate value system, then whenever anything arises in our meditation that is considered negative we deem our meditation a failure or regression. Indeed, we deem ourselves a failure. If we measure our worth in meditation by our capacity to quiet and control our minds, we feel triumphant and validated by our capacity to quell disturbing elements within ourselves.

In the course of an intensive meditation retreat, it is not uncommon for a participant to feel full of self-congratulation upon being able to count fifty breaths in a row or remain without thought for one minute. Yet there is no inherent distinction in being able to quiet our minds. And the capacity to watch an uninterrupted sequence of breathing is no qualification for worthiness. Nor does it necessarily qualify us to live with wisdom, sensitivity, or compassion.

If we use detachment as a yardstick for our spiritual progress, we may find ourselves censoring our responses, reprimanding ourselves for laughter or delight, feeling that we have fallen and regressed in our cultivation of detachment. Cautioned to guard our sense doors against the lure of sensuality, we may view ourselves as being spiritually inadequate when our hearts respond to the song of a bird or the beauty of a dawn sky. Just as our grandmothers constricted their bodies with corsets and stays in the name of sanctioned social values, we can equally constrict and inhibit our spiritual creativity and freedom in the name of unquestioned spiritual values.

When we set up rigid guidelines for spiritual worthiness, we find ourselves constantly seeking for signs of either progress or regression, correspondingly feeling either gratified or depressed when we find them. Our spirituality, or our image of it, becomes yet another means by which we judge and measure ourselves. Our denial or acceptance of ourselves is once more dependent upon our capacity to conform to models and value systems we have absorbed and adopted out of fear and a belief in our powerlessness. We project power on to those models and values, and then define the very worth of our being by the standards we have created. As long as we continue to be alienated from inner wisdom, we will repeat this pattern of being dependent upon feedback for our sense of worthiness and repeat the experience of feeling spineless in the face of feedback—even when the source of that feedback is our own thoughts and projections.

Our meditation takes on the color of our own unique patterns of relationship, and it can become shaded with brutality if we transfer patterns of self-negation to our spiritual exploration. We judge, punish, undermine, and suppress ourselves as we label ourselves: good or bad; worthy or unworthy. Our standards of failure and success become the scourges with which we abuse ourselves.

On discovering that her partner was involved in a clandestine relationship with another woman, Ellen found herself filled with feelings of betrayal, anger, and jealousy. She interpreted these feelings as being confirmations of her spiritual inadequacy. She believed that if she truly had any measure of spiritual evolvement, she would be able to experience more forgiveness and acceptance instead of such a torrent of negativity. She felt that the years she had dedicated to her spiritual growth had been a waste. The despair she experienced over the breakup of her relationship was matched by the despair she experienced over being a spiritual failure.

The vision of the spiritual warrior, who cuts through the negative, uproots impurities, and disciplines the mind and body in a martial way, is just one of the images and concepts that can be used to affirm a misuse of power. The effects of using power to control remain the same: pain, fragmentation, alienation, and fear. It is all too easy to mistake suppression and control for transcendence. Our energy and power can be utilized to control our minds, subdue our feelings, and withdraw from our bodies. They can also be utilized to call forth the fertility that all aspects of our being have the potential to offer for enriching our spiritual growth and wholeness. When we begin to accept that our anger and grief are as valid a source of learning as our quietness and detachment, we begin to accept ourselves, to heal ourselves, and to transform ourselves.

If we have come to experience life from the perspective of being powerless, overwhelmed and overpowered by people, things, and events—we find ourselves living out this pattern in our spiritual practices as well. We may subject ourselves to the power of others, perhaps selecting teachers, spiritual practices, religions, or sects who will gladly tell us what to do and how to do it, in great detail. In doing so, we have the solace of inhabiting a world made safe by order and regimentation. Our dress, language, lifestyle, belief systems, and ways of relating are standardized by the authority of a tradition or teacher.

Meinrad Craighead writes in *Immanent Mother,*

> For fourteen years I lived out the Christian life within a monastic context. My gradual disillusionment with monastic life and my unease grew in proportion to my realization of my sisters' narrow and rigid expectations of what that life should be. The community mind sought the survival of a social and spiritual tradition. I thought monastic life was about freedom of spirit and the risks of an unorthodox life. For most of the nuns, the enclosed life ensured the continuation of the inherited security of English homes and institutions, which had conditioned them to play expected roles. The monastery offered no possibility of escaping this conditioning; indeed the life continually reinforced it. Although I desired to live a monastic life, I could not do so among dependent, inauthentic people estranged from themselves. I often had the feeling of living among ghosts absorbed in playing roles in one repetitive script, acting in order to receive acceptance and approval.[5]

Conformity is rewarded by approval and affirmation, whereas doubt is dismissed as being a lack of experience or spiritual depth, and disregarded. Within sanctioned religious communities we find, without doubt, women who are able to utilize their creativity fully and expand their sense of inner freedom. They are women who have understood and resolved their fears and insecurities in relationship to authority and approval and are thus free to utilize the monastic life as the framework for the life of the spirit and not as an end in itself.

In meditation, we may find we are overwhelmed by our thoughts, memories, sensations, and images. We turn our attention inward, only to feel bombarded by an onslaught of thought and imagery endlessly recycling unwanted or irrelevant data that tire and distress us. We may feel helpless before it, and it is easier to control and suppress these data than to confront and understand the vacuum of inner alienation and discontent that creates this endless mentality. One retreat participant communicated to me his despondency when upon turning his attention inward to discover his "true self," he discovered his true self seemed to be no more than a jukebox end-lessly programmed to recycle the records of his past. We can call upon our willpower to discipline and control our minds but in doing so create both inner fragmentation and pressure.

Holding models of what a spiritual person is—an endless sunbeam of love, generosity, and patience—we feel helpless in the face of our high expec-tations, models, and standards and in our inability to attain them. We look inward for peace, compassion, and clarity. We feel despondent when we dis-cover chaos, disharmony, and confusion. We come to feel inadequate, unable to bring about any real inner change. Disdaining our own worth, we turn outward once more to find identity, approval, and affirmation. Doubt-ing ourselves, we become dependent once more on the opinions and affir-mation of others for our own sense of spiritual worth and accomplishment. We gain approval by relinquishing inner trust and reliance upon our own experience, substituting the adoption of values, goals, patterns, and activi-ties provided by others.

To move from darkness into light, we need to be willing to embrace the twilight within—the times of disillusionment with ourselves; the chaos and disorder—and sustain our inner exploration. We empower ourselves not only by discovering resources of joy, peace, and wisdom within, but also by cultivating the strength and dedication to move through our own distress and discontent. Our trust in ourselves is strengthened when we experien-tially understand that we have the inner resources to withstand being over-powered, whether the source of that domination is outside or within ourselves.

At times, the feeling of powerlessness is dressed up in spiritual garb and called humility, in a misunderstanding of the true meaning of the word. We can learn to feel pride in self-negation through calling it selflessness. We learn to justify withdrawal and defensiveness through calling it detachment. Concepts are manipulated to disguise our own fear and misuse of power. While I was practicing in the East, I was invited to address the monastery, to give a discourse on some aspect of spirituality. It was also suggested that this would be an ideal opportunity to express my own humility by sitting in the shadows in the corner rather than standing at the podium to deliver my talk, because the monks would be offended by having a woman stand above them. My refusal to participate in the arrangement was interpreted as an indication of my pride and lack of understanding of the validity of the rules of ordination, which called upon women to assume a subservient position.

We have the freedom to consent to or dissent from established power centers and value systems when we deeply understand that nothing in the present has the power to condition us, to overwhelm us, or to undermine us, unless we are alienated from an inner power and trust and thus give our power away. Agnes Martin, an elder stateswoman of American painters, remarks, "Now we must consider the idea of power, because without freedom we cannot make our full response. With the idea of power in our minds, we are subject to that power. If you believe in it, then you are subject to it. But in reality there is no power anywhere."

The practice of spirituality and of meditation is, in a very real sense, learning to empower ourselves, but in radically different ways than we have previously experienced. It is learning to discover new sources of power in ourselves that are qualitatively different from the sources of power we have become accustomed to. It is learning to trust in our own capacity for change and transformation through reclaiming our own power to direct and create the quality of our lives and being. It is power that is rooted in inner wisdom and sensitivity.

Meditation begins simply by being with oneself without the authority of anyone or anything to dictate what or how we should be. We focus our attention intimately upon this state of aloneness, without goals, expectations, or images, and thus can actually connect with who we are in the moment and the changes taking place within. By cultivating attention, we empower ourselves, for the capacity to focus clearly is the capacity to free our consciousness from the distortions of our own conditioning and from outer undermining influences.

Clarity of focus enables us to see what contributes to our well-being and wholeness and what undermines it. Clarity of focus allows our own creativity to unfold and frees us to respond to the world and to ourselves from a place of wisdom and sensitivity.

With clear attention, there is born a greater sense of spaciousness within, an enhanced awareness, which nurtures the growth of trust, openness, and sensitivity. The very things that may have threatened to overpower or overwhelm us previously no longer do so. Not because we can now control them, not because we have rid ourselves of anything, and not because we have improved ourselves, but simply through the empowerment born of being clearly and sensitively present in the moment. The experience of being overwhelmed by our minds is minimized, and with the deepening of inner connection comes a greater effectiveness in every area of our lives.

Donna's fear of people had been an ever-present shadow in her life. She felt locked in an endless quandary of feeling either the victim of others or ensnared by an inner need to dominate and master others. Acting on this fear, her attention was constantly focused upon assessing the responses of others. Taking time to be alone, learning to be present with herself and her own responses, she discovered that it was possible for her to step out of this repetitive cycle of reaction and that she could act and respond from a place of inner clarity and sensitivity.

The unfolding of inner wisdom radiates outward to transform our actions, relationships, and sense of connection with all life. Experiencing a different quality of attention toward our energies, memories, feelings, expectations, and sensations, we learn at the deepest level that we need be neither a victim nor a master. We truly understand that if we no longer cast ourselves in the role of the victim of our own conditioning and mind, there is nothing in this world that can victimize us. This understanding allows us to create new relationships with people and events that formerly overwhelmed us or that we found ourselves compelled to control.

If meditation is approached with care, sensitivity, gentleness, and curiosity, we discover within ourselves the power of love, the love of being. Directing that love inward has a powerful and transforming effect on our being. Freedom from self-degradation, self-hatred, and a sense of worthlessness brings with it a dramatic transformation of our vision of ourselves and of life. We learn that we do not have to become anything, deny anything, or, above all, become perfect: our freedom is not dependent upon becoming perfect. Just by consciously being with what is actually unfolding within ourselves, with love and sensitivity, learning evolves and wisdom emerges. Our love for, and acceptance of, our own being are the foundation for every other relationship, empowering us to transform not only our own being but also our world.

With the capacity to be with ourselves comes immense strength, the strength of balance, clarity, and attention. It is the strength of not needing to protect, not needing to avoid, not needing to control, and not needing to be safe or hide from ourselves. Learning how to be alone in a fruitful, exploratory way rather than in alienation or disconnection nurtures a true sense of wholeness and completeness. The need for approval or winning to measure our worth drops away, and we are free of dependency.

We must look carefully at what is taking place in our relationship to ourselves and our lives: are we struggling, are we resisting, or are we indulging (which are expressions of powerlessness)? Are we censoring, are we judging, or are we avoiding (expressions of seeking power over)? Do we have a cooperative relationship with our resistance, anger, grief, sadness, joy, and connection? Do we have a cooperative relationship with our bodies, feelings, thoughts, and dreams?

A cooperative relationship is a clear recognition that everything is a vehicle for learning and for understanding. Each moment brings us messages for learning if there is a cooperative relationship with the moment, which is a relationship of sensitivity, receptivity, openness, and strength.

When we no longer struggle to conform to an image of spiritual perfection, meditation can be a celebration. When we can be with what is in a clear, strong, and loving way, transformation comes very spontaneously. Peace and compassion are not goals to be striven for, but qualities that spontaneously emerge from a consciousness that is peaceful and compassionate. In that spontaneous emergence, we find strength in our own power and trust in our own sources of power, so that we may live in a clear, meaningful, loving, and free way.

## Meditation on Inner Empowerment • • •

Settle yourself into a posture that is relaxed. Let your whole body relax; let your mind relax. Let your breathing deepen and soothe your entire body. Let your breath caress any areas of tension you feel. Let your breath relax and find its own rhythm and depth. Feel the stillness and calmness of your body.

From the top of your head, let your attention slowly move down through your body. Mentally touch each part of your body, embracing it with loving attention. As you move your attention down through your body, silently acknowledge the power and life of each area of your body.

Let your attention touch your eyes, and acknowledge that these eyes you touch are the doors through which you receive the world. The ears you touch are the doors that enable you to listen to the sounds of life. With your mouth you can speak the words of truth and love that enrich the world you share. With your lips you can smile and articulate that which is meaningful to you.

Continue that loving, gentle movement of attention down through your body. Your chest embraces and responds to the movement of your breath and your life. Your breasts hold the potential to nourish. Your womb is the source of all life. With your arms you can embrace the world with love and compassion. Your hands can touch with sensitivity, can create so much of beauty and wonder.

Caress your legs with your attention: they are your vehicles for running and for dancing. With your feet you connect with the Earth beneath you. Let yourself feel your whole body. Embrace your body with love and sensitivity, feeling its life, its energy, and its power. Embrace any areas of tension or holding with that same sensitivity. Feel them release and relax. Let yourself appreciate the power and the vitality of your body. Let yourself merge with the loving attention that is your own vehicle for bonding with yourself and with the world.

Bring into your mind, and your heart, a feeling or a thought about yourself that is difficult for you to accept. Feelings of unworthiness, resentment, powerlessness, or anger: none of these is an easy feeling for us to integrate. As you hold that feeling in your awareness, feel how you respond to that feeling. Feel any contraction, denial, or avoidance that emerges. Be aware of any judgments or condemnations that arise. Surround your feelings, your reactions, with loving attention. Let your heart open to them: let yourself soften around them.

Let yourself feel the pain of contraction, of denial. Let yourself feel the pain of self-judgment. Open your heart to those feelings, and surround them with loving spaciousness. Feel them change as you embrace those feelings with loving kindness. Feel them soften: see the freedom in loving kindness, in letting go. Know that you don't have to be bound by denial: see how the blocks of fear and unworthiness are transformed by your loving attention, transformed by your own loving kindness.

Bring your attention to settle into your heart area. Fill that space with love, with sensitivity, and with warmth. Let it expand to fill your whole being. Let it expand to fill the space around you to embrace all of life. Feel the energy and the power of your loving kindness and your sensitivity. Feel the pain of all those who are blocked by fear or denial. Feel the pain of all those who are alienated from love. Touch that pain with the vastness of your own loving kindness. Let yourself touch the heart of all life. Let yourself bathe in your own loving kindness, and let it transform you. Feel the peace and the compassion of your love.

# Chapter 6
## *Spiritual Resources*

O UR VISION of ourselves, whether conscious or unconscious, is the foundation of our identities, our actions, and the choices we make in our lives. This vision has a direct influence on our own sense of possibility and potential. Our ability to bring about change, both outwardly and inwardly, is directly related to this vision. Our own sense of power and our capacity for transformation are enhanced or limited by the vision that we hold of who we are. Whether we reach for horizons or for boundaries, for freedom or for safety, these are choices clearly influenced by the sense of inner vision we embrace.

Yet it may be rare that we take the time or give attention to deeply questioning who we are. It is a difficult question. It can also be a very frightening question, because this questioning necessarily brings forth our whole sense of being into consciousness. It is somehow easier, at times more attractive, to drift through life avoiding this question, or being defined by someone or something else. The lessons of our lives tell us that the implications of awareness are far reaching: awareness spells questioning, at times challenge, at times change, always honesty. These ingredients of awareness also spell anxiety to us if we live with a wounded inner vision.

When we ask ourselves who we are, we answer ourselves with concepts or labels that are often no more than descriptions of the credentials or limitations we identify with. You may define yourself by your function or profession. You may describe yourself by your relationship: I'm gay, I'm straight, I'm married, I'm a mother, or I'm single. You may tend to define yourself by your personality. You may say that you are anxious or aggressive, that you are extroverted or defensive, or that you are alienated or trusting. Or you may describe yourself by your feelings: I am emotional, I feel inadequate, I feel worthy, or I feel powerful. You may find yourself rooted in one or all of these different modes of being.

Whatever first comes into your mind can give you a fairly accurate indication of your way of experiencing the world, for this experience is governed by your vision of who you are. If we feel ourselves to be powerless, we experience the world as an entity that threatens to consume or overwhelm us. If we feel ourselves to be angry, we experience the world as an adversary, hostile to our survival. If we believe ourselves to be inadequate, we experience the world in a way quite different from that experienced by someone who feels herself to be powerful.

Sometimes the roots of our inner vision are unconscious. Earlier in this book, I delineated the cycle of conditioning that occurs in every life, a process that begins long before we are aware of what is going on. Starting at a very early age, the expectations, beliefs, values, and standards of others are absorbed; then they are internalized; and finally, they become unconscious. If we repeat something often enough within ourselves, it becomes a truth. An unconscious inner vision is the most lethal vision that it is possible to hold, because, essentially, our lives are simply the enactment of the expectations of others. Our very being becomes dedicated to conformity, to safety, and to acceptability. Our life can become a mission committed to pleasing others.

Tanya aptly describes the puppetlike existence decreed by an inner vision that is unconscious:

> I approached everything in my life—my relationships, my educational choices, my work, and my identity—like a good team player. Before I started anything, I had to know the field, the goals, and the rules, and I could begin only if I was assured of joining the winning team. I equated doing things right with being right and winning with being worthy. I always played by the rules, because to digress meant to become an outcast, and nothing was worse to me than failure or banishment. I played a lot of games, winning a few and losing too many, before it finally dawned on me that I had never truly elected to join any of those teams or play any of those games. What a liberation when my resistance to being a pawn finally overwhelmed my reluctance to take responsibility for my own life!

We cannot help but enact our internalized beliefs. We cannot help but enact and express our vision of who we are, be it conscious or unconscious. If we believe ourselves to be needy, we will find ourselves going through life seeking protection and tying our umbilical cord to the most promising womb. If we believe ourselves to be inadequate or worthless, we will make sure that we do not aspire to anything too high in our lives. When we do fail to bring about changes we wish for or to reach a goal we aspire to, we won't be surprised. We will feel a sense of familiarity: *Yes, it's happened again. It's the way I am.*

If we feel ourselves to be unlovable, we will find ourselves again and again in relationships that undermine our sense of worth and reinforce our sense of being unlovable. Again and again, we will experience rejection, loneliness, and alienation—almost as if we were seeking it out! If we believe ourselves to be incomplete, lacking in wholeness inwardly, we will repeatedly establish power centers outside of ourselves, in authorities and people who will tell us who to be and how to live.

The effects of having a negative unconscious vision of ourselves are extreme frustration and pain. Yet it is so hard to let go of such a vision precisely because it is unconscious and therefore inaccessible to us. We are unable to learn from the lessons of our lives, and our experience of the present becomes only a repetition of the past. We feel helpless to bring about change. We feel powerless and resentful.

At other times, we are afraid of changing. Change means entering unfamiliar territory and embracing the unknown. We may feel quite justified in not taking a risk, thereby losing what support and affirmation we already have. We may feel more comfortable within a cocoon of safety even if we lack fulfillment or wholeness. Jeanette visited a monastery, responding to an inner call for a more contemplative life. She was directed to the nuns' quarters and joined in their daily routines. After a few days, she found she no longer wanted to ignore the undercurrents of unrest and discontent she sensed among a number of the nuns. One evening, she decided to ask the nuns what it was all about. Several of them gave voice to a number of different concerns. They spoke of the conflict they felt between wanting to be a nun yet also feeling they were sacrificing their dignity and integrity through their subservience to the monks, the conflict between wanting to be selfless yet not be devoid of self-respect. They also spoke of the guilt they felt over their discontent: the discontent being proof of their inability to transcend such worldly concerns. One of the nuns had become increasingly restless during the discussion and finally blurted out, "This is just your mind talking. Isn't our practice to overcome our clinging and our thoughts? There's only one way to be a nun and stay here, and that's by letting go." For the rest of her days in the monastery, Jeanette was virtually ignored by the nuns.

Our vision of ourselves may be conscious: this does not mean that it is free of distortion. A distorted conscious vision can handicap us in our lives just as an unconscious vision does. We may feel deeply angry within ourselves and hostile in our relationship to life. We may believe that we are not only justified in our anger but that we are wise and realistic to be angry. Our anger may be rooted in repeated experiences of being exploited. The conclusion we draw is that the world is truly a hostile environment to live in and that we must protect ourselves with our anger.

Experiences of exploitation or abuse inevitably leave behind traces of pain and fear. These residues may express themselves in the present in a feeling of being both fragile and vulnerable. That vulnerability takes the form of suspicion as to the motives and integrity of others. The message we have concluded on the basis of our past experiences is that we are fully justified in being on guard against others.

There is validity in the idea of protecting ourselves. To go through life feeling that everything is acceptable is not an expression of openness but of naiveté. But we need to be wary of subscribing to a vision that is founded upon isolating any one experience, for such a vision may not necessarily be true. When wounded by a negative experience, we easily form conclusions about ourselves and the world. Our conclusions become the truth we believe in. We come to inhabit a personal reality that is tied to the past. As Jessica put it, "My last rejection finally taught me that I never want to experience such betrayal again. I can't trust anyone. I won't trust anyone." In essence, a scar is formed. When we see this happening to ourselves, we must remind ourselves that scar tissue is dead. We cannot grow or open ourselves to our own possibilities as long as we are tied to and subscribe to a wounded vision of ourselves. In assuming a stance of defensiveness to protect ourselves against fear and pain, we equally deny ourselves the realization and fulfillment of our own potential.

Is it possible for us to leave behind a wounded and fragmented vision of ourselves? How can we begin to heal and bring forth change? To take the first step toward inner wholeness and freedom, we are called upon to distinguish within ourselves the difference between the true and the false, and through that understanding, be able to discard all falseness and falsehood in every area of our lives. Nurturing an inner vision that is liberating is a twofold process. It is a process of discovering who we are, and it is a process of discovering who we are not. It is beginning to understand what is true within ourselves and what is untrue. It is a process of questioning the very roots of our inner vision and whether our vision of ourselves in this moment is based upon truth or untruth.

Within the process of meditation in which we develop a finely tuned and gentle inner listening, a series of dynamics begins to become apparent. It is not helpful to reduce ourselves to a series of psychological dynamics, yet it is important to acknowledge the influence and power our inner dynamics have upon us. It is also important to identify the various values assigned to these dynamics and the power these values possess to condition our vision of ourselves.

We hold within ourselves the capacity to reason, alongside the capacity to feel. Within our culture, these two elements are assigned very distinct and separate values. Reason is generally considered to be a "masculine" value; feeling is given the label "feminine." (When I refer to the masculine or the feminine, I do not refer to those qualities as specifically belonging to one sex rather than another. Rather, I use those references as evocative terms.) The capacity to reason, to be rational, and to be intellectual is awarded a great deal of respect and prestige in our society. So many of the social, scholastic, and professional goals that are deemed to be significant actually depend upon our capacity to analyze, conceptualize, reason, and plan.

The companion to our reasoning capacity is our capacity to feel emotion and the power of its presence within ourselves and our lives. In our culture, emotion is something that is frequently regarded with a certain amount of suspicion and anxiety. If we look back on our lives, we will probably recognize that as women we have a tendency to neutralize our emotions. Emotion is often regarded as a hindrance to action and to rationality. Emotion is also frequently, and erroneously, regarded as weakness.

With our minds, we plan the future, conceptualize about the present, and analyze the past. With our minds, we also articulate and express who we are. With our minds, we are able to cultivate the power of attention, of focus, of direction.

With our hearts and through our emotions, we learn how to give and how to receive. We learn how to form bonds and how to sustain relationships. Within our hearts, we experience the extremes of love and despair. Within our hearts and feelings, we also store our rejections, our wounds, our pain, and our alienation. Within our hearts, we can feel compassionate and connected. Within our hearts, we can also feel painfully alienated and alone. Through the very medium of our emotions, we feel intuitive.

With the power of our minds, we can order and we can organize. We can also control and learn how to quiet ourselves. It is that capacity to order and control that is valued highly. Our minds are often regarded as reliable, strong, and rational. These values, so glibly attributed to our minds, are directly questioned by anyone who takes even a few hours to sit quietly alone without external input.

The kind of order that our minds can create we rarely find within our emotions. Instead, what we find is turbulence and immense power. We find that we love and that we hate, that we feel joy, that we feel sorrow. We discover depths of anger and feeling. They are intense. They are vital. Looking at the intensity and the extremes of our emotions, we may conclude—or have it concluded for us—that our emotional life, the life of our feelings, is unreliable and not to be trusted, just as the power of our intuition is easily dismissed as fanciful thinking.

We bring both our minds and our hearts to spirituality. We encounter some very familiar values in relation to them. In the context of spiritual development, the importance of developing detachment, quietness, and equanimity is stressed. Those qualities are valid for, and needed by, most of us. We experience that we can develop the power and capacity of our minds to bring about this detachment, quietness, and equanimity. It is, however, very important that we question what it is we are trying to detach ourselves from and why we are doing so.

Our detachment may be skillful, or it may be aimed at learning how to separate ourselves not only from the disorder and power of our feelings and emotions, but also from the feelings themselves. The anxiety and mistrust we feel concerning our emotions find their justification in spirituality, in developing a spiritual path that leads to inner calm. Basically, there comes about a misinterpretation of detachment: detachment becomes a means of controlling the emotions that arise within us.

The capacity to order, to organize, and to achieve quietness can appear an attractive goal. It also appears a logical endeavor to undertake. Indeed, many women find themselves valuing order and organization highly. At one time or another, all of us have experienced what it feels like to be overwhelmed by emotion. Being overpowered by feeling can leave us in a position in which we feel extremely weak and vulnerable. I use the term "weak" because the experience of being overwhelmed by emotion places us in a position in which it becomes quite difficult, if not impossible, to articulate or to express what we are actually feeling.

Too often, we find ourselves in a situation where our feelings tell us that something is amiss and yet the very strength of those feelings makes it difficult for us to express or pinpoint the problem. At such times, we find ourselves intimidated by the rationality of those who use logic as a weapon. We may be accused of just reacting, or just being emotional, or not making sense. It may be pointed out to us that if there were any truth in what we felt, we would surely be able to express it in a way that others could understand. Confronted by such logic, we easily find ourselves floundering in our emotions. Unable to prove or articulate the validity of our inner experience, we may find ourselves doubting its truth. If we experience this intimidation repeatedly, we learn that to be overpowered by our own emotions is equal to being overpowered by others' logic. We may find ourselves becoming silenced by our own doubt and our fear of being overpowered.

Charlotte spoke about the positive feedback she received from so many of her co-workers and from several of the teachers who guided her spiritual life:

> Everyone praises me for my quietness and humility. I rarely disagree. I rarely threaten anyone by challenging them. I wasn't always like this. I feel very vulnerable with others. I seem to sense so easily the power plays in relationships, the undercurrents of anger, defensiveness, and anxiety. I used to ask people about them. So often I was accused of projecting my own feelings on to them, of being wrong. I don't really believe I was or am always wrong. I've learned to be quiet, to stifle my

perceptions, to hide my vulnerability. It's too painful to be honest.

We may find ourselves attracted to being logical and rational. We feel we are more in control, both of ourselves and of the encounters in which we find ourselves, when able to conceptualize about and express intellectually what we are experiencing. Yet at war with that attraction is the instinctive value that we give to the very intensity of our feelings. We may feel elated; we may feel sorrowful. We may feel passionate; we may feel anxious. We are also very conscious that within those extremes of feelings we do actually feel. There is vitality, there is life. And there is connection, both inward and outward. We know that the connection with our own feelings opens us in a way in which we can be touched and moved by the joy and the pain of the world we live in.

There is resistance to losing that bonding and vitality despite our attraction to rationality. The loss of the connection with the vitality and acuteness of our own feelings entails an inner life that is sterile. We may feel that our capacity to reason and our capacity to feel are contradictory, if not opposed to each other. There is a lack of rapport between the two and a concomitant sense of inner fragmentation. This lack of wholeness, in turn, has a profound effect on our lives.

It is a friction that brings discord into the professional, spiritual, and intimate lives of so many women. The professional woman who feels she must adopt the qualities and characteristics of her male colleagues if she is to be able to compete; the woman in the religious life who feels she must sacrifice her femininity in order to be accepted as a worthy aspirant; and the woman in a relationship who feels she is compelled to display only her femininity in order to maintain the relationship: all are expressions of the conflict we experience between our intellect and our heart.

We may value rationality because it appears to bring safety from turmoil. At the same time, we recognize and value the vitality and intensity that emotions and feelings give to our lives. We may fear the consequences of our emotions; equally, we shrink from an inner life that is devoid of feeling. Rarely do we feel a cooperative relationship or rapport between these dynamics.

The capacity for reason and the capacity for emotion are inner dynamics that can be either creative or destructive. With the power of our minds we can cultivate attention, bringing clarity and focus. These are powers that, when employed wisely and skillfully, enable us to articulate and express all that we feel. Through attention, we cultivate the capacity to be present and the capacity to be conscious. It is not a capacity that should then be used to help us avoid our feelings and emotions. Rather, it is a capacity that enables us to be wisely present with our feelings and emotions in a way that is free of distortion, free of prejudice, and free of inner judgment.

The capacity to be attentive is one that becomes destructive if it degenerates through fear. It degenerates when we are driven by the desire to protect ourselves from all the implications of connection. Our perspective can degenerate into distance; our detachment can degenerate into control; and our quietness can degenerate into suppression. In that process of degeneration, what we are basically attempting to do is to create an oasis within ourselves in which we feel safe and undisturbed.

In the process of cultivating distance, control, and a quietness that rests upon suppression, we disown very large parts of ourselves. We attempt to disown the sources of turmoil as we perceive them: our bodies and our emotions. The end result of disowning them is that we become dispossessed of them. In being dispossessed, we cannot learn through the vehicle of our emotions. In our dismissal of them, we cannot utilize our capacity to feel as a vehicle for being increasingly conscious and awake.

The process of inner exploration involves developing an acute awareness of the changes and movements that take place within ourselves on a moment-to-moment level. We may assure ourselves of the quality of our awareness through the precision with which we are able to watch and observe our inner changes. Anger arises; as we place upon it the keenness of our observation, it disappears. Sorrow, elation, despair, and joy are all dissolved by the power of our watching. A natural evolvement of meditation is the cultivating of an inner spaciousness and openness in which we are not overwhelmed by the feelings and thoughts that arise within. Their very power is neutralized by the tranquility and awareness that receive them.

We do also need to appreciate that our very watching and observation can also carry with them the motivation and intention to disarm feelings, because they threaten to disturb and challenge the very tranquility we cherish. In quietness, we find safety and control, experiences we consciously or unconsciously value highly. When motivated by the desire to be undisturbed above all else, our watching becomes a tool to deny and avoid the emotions that threaten disturbance. Spiritually, we lobotomize ourselves.

Denial and avoidance are not means to understanding or integration. They are means only to suppression and disconnection. We pay the price in the escalation of inner tension and pressure. Joanna described how she was a fervent devotee of the practice of suppression:

> I loved to go on intensive retreats, the longer and the more silent they were, the better I liked them. I really had a hard time coming out, having to talk to people, having to manage my life. I felt assaulted inwardly and outwardly every time I left a retreat by my own feelings and my need to respond to other people. I could hardly wait to go into another retreat. I could get so quiet when I could do nothing but sit and watch. I felt really insulted by one of my teachers, when after describing my experience to him, he suggested that I was involved in the pursuit of safety rather than understanding. His suggestion that I was using my spirituality to avoid myself and life really offended me. I felt I deserved praise for being such a good watcher, not blame. Now I feel grateful to him. It was true. My inner life is not so quiet any more, but in feeling the pulse of my own life I also feel the pulse of everything.

When our capacity for attention degenerates through fear or through the desire for safety, we engage in a spirituality that is defensive. We enact an idea of spirituality that basically denies our inner experience. Using this kind of unskillful attention to protect ourselves from our own experience of who we are, our detachment becomes withdrawal from both the inner and the outer world.

There are clear symptoms that express the degeneration of attention. First of all, we find ourselves censoring all the time. Our meditation and inner observation are used as a watchdog and judge of what we actually experience, rather than as an appreciation of and openness to our inner experience. We find that we hold some clearly defined values that determine what a valid experience is. We may find ourselves experiencing a strong emotion of happiness, or even sorrow, which is then followed by a feeling of guilt or shame. We feel we have been indulgent or weak in experiencing the emotion. We feel we have lost our detachment and must watch more closely. We may find ourselves censoring our responses to life and to ourselves. Our delight in seeing a flower unfolding is followed by doubt in the validity of that feeling. We censure ourselves for becoming involved or for reacting. Our responses are reduced to being signs of failure. Naomi expressed the delight she felt in seeing the colors of the sunset, the trees outlined on the horizon. The response she received was, "It's no more than name and form: it's empty. You're coloring it with your own desire for gratification."

A woman whose mother had recently died once attended a retreat. She was in the midst of grieving, feeling a deep sense of loss and devastation. Her ability to grieve and to integrate the feelings she was experiencing was blocked by the conceptual spiritual burden she carried. She felt it was not spiritual to grieve: rather, it was a sign of her attachment that she had not yet renounced. She firmly believed that if she were truly developed in her spiritual life, then she would just be able to let go. She interpreted her own sadness as a sign of inadequacy. She grieved not for her mother alone, but for the loss of her own spiritual self-image.

We know the power of our emotions. The power of our emotions can be destructive. We know what it feels like to be overwhelmed by self-judgment. We know what it feels like to be overwhelmed by feelings of inadequacy. We know the pain of depression. We know, too, the power of joy, of love, and of empathy. We need to acknowledge the place of the power of our emotions. Our emotions connect us with the life of our world, with the heart of our own being. Without feeling, there is no connection. Without feeling, how can we care either for our world or for ourselves? Our capacity to form bonds of connectedness with all of life is based upon our capacity to touch our own hearts and the hearts of others. That capacity to bond, to connect, and to utilize our feelings in a wise way is a power that is truly significant in every area of our lives, including our spiritual life.

We need the power of our minds to cultivate attention and clarity, not so that we can withdraw from our emotions, but so that we can be fully present with them and articulate them. We need to develop detachment so that we can set aside the conditioned values that label emotions weakness. Detachment, the capacity to observe gently, involves cultivating an inner environment in which there is true spaciousness, rather than a fabricated quietness. In this environment, our feelings can emerge without our being overwhelmed or overpowered by them. Clarity of attention empowers us to focus rather than flounder, to utilize our emotions rather than be submerged by them. In cultivating a rapport between our minds and our hearts, we perceive that emotion is not a weakness but truly a strength.

How can we care for our planet and for one another unless we can be deeply moved and touched? Who will care, apart from ourselves, through opening our own hearts? The power of our emotions can be used creatively to bond and to transform. The power of love, the power of healing, and the power of compassion are rooted in our capacity to feel, to be touched and to touch the hearts of others. If the power of our emotions is in rapport with our minds, we have a clear channel of articulation that expresses the potential for love, healing, and compassion we hold within.

Much of the suffering that devastates our planet is rooted not only in our incapacity to feel, but also in our unwillingness to appreciate the consequences of that incapacity. Economies are founded upon greed and exploitation. Governments concern themselves with power plays. Politicians barter with one another over minor reductions in their nuclear arsenals. In the busyness of all this posturing, bartering, and plotting, where is the heart and the space to truly appreciate the consequences of our fear and greed? In the busyness of balancing our ledgers and producing our statistics, can we truly feel what it would mean to see our world devastated? The children who would die are our children. The world that would be extinguished is the world that supports and nurtures us.

The blocking of our capacity to feel, the degeneration of focus into distance and withdrawal, is a disconnection from our capacity to transform our world and ourselves with love and compassion. So much superficiality and conflict are dissolved in the light of our interconnectedness and mutual dependency. The place of our emotions, our hearts, needs to be acknowledged, not just in our spiritual lives but in the whole of our lives.

Previously, I quoted Solomon Ibn Gavirol : "Of what avail is an open eye if the heart is blind?" We, too, need to ask ourselves, *Of what avail are our knowledge, our theories and our concepts if we do not know how to open our hearts to ourselves and to others?*

We cultivate clarity not to be less emotional, not to quell our feelings. Instead, we cultivate clarity so that our emotions and the very power of our feelings can emerge and be articulated in ways that can heal, both inwardly and outwardly. We cultivate clarity to bring about a rapport between our minds and our hearts. This rapport in no way diminishes our feminine identity, but deepens our sense of being awake, aware, and whole women.

The qualities of strength and vulnerability in relation to each other form a pattern that is analogous to reason and feeling. Strength is a quality that usually carries with it the association of being masculine; vulnerability is generally deemed a feminine quality. If we look within ourselves, we see that we have the capacity to be strong; equally, we are capable of being deeply vulnerable. Strength is also used as a weapon against vulnerability. It is the preferred and desired mode. There is a need to be strong, but I do not mean the kind of strength associated with overpowering others or even aspects of ourselves, which is how strength is generally defined. We need the strength that is born of inner connection and empowerment.

When we are alienated from our inner strength, this very belief in our powerlessness invites exploitation and abuse. We will find ourselves being repeatedly undermined and debilitated, not only by others but also by the force of our own conditioning. Alienated from inner strength, we also find ourselves violating our own integrity. Feeling bereft of any firm ground to stand upon inwardly, we make compromises that we regret. We capitulate to the expectations and demands of others even when knowing intuitively that our capitulation is one that demeans our integrity. If we believe ourselves to be weak, our lives become not an expression of the truths we understand, but an act of surrender to anything that appears to be stronger than ourselves. Feeling alienated from our inner strength, we find ourselves being dictated to constantly by outside authorities, by people, by situations, or being overwhelmed by our inner experience.

Natasha succinctly described the experience of believing herself to be empty of strength:

> I always needed and wanted someone to look up to and to hide behind. I exchanged my mother for a teacher, a teacher for a boyfriend, a boyfriend for a husband, and a husband for membership in a religious sect. I dedicated my whole life to finding an infallible pillar of strength. I knew it didn't exist within me. I lived in hope that it existed somewhere, anywhere else. It was terrifying for me to discover

that I couldn't find a lasting sanctuary anywhere. It was when I was forced, through endless disappointment, to examine myself more closely that I began to understand that the emptiness I had so much feared within me was fuller than I would ever have believed possible.

To be strong is to be powerful. To be strong is to be effective. To be strong is also to be energetic and persistent. In our search to discover an authentic spiritual vision, we need that strength. We are surrounded by so many authorities who will dispense goals, who will dispense expectations, and who will dispense images of who we should be and become. We need strength so that we can draw upon the richness of others' experience and yet not feel compelled to conform or violate our own integrity. For women who step outside the paths and systems of sanctioned religion, that strength is even more essential. Devoting ourselves to a spiritual life that is outside the boundaries of traditional spirituality, we may lose the assurance of having familiar signposts to guide us. There may be no authority beyond ourselves to praise us for making progress or to encourage us in moments of doubt.

Several times in my own meditation training, I was cautioned not to cultivate particular states of consciousness, because they were not a part of the path a particular teacher recommended. I was warned not to cultivate particular practices because they did not conform to the guidelines of yet another teacher. At those times, I had nowhere to turn but to myself, to question whether my wish to follow particular directions was born of stubbornness, or of pride, or of an intuitive sense that those directions were pertinent to my own inner development.

If we consciously tread a spiritual path that is not defined for us, we must also accept that we consciously dispense with the affirmation and reassurance of others. We travel a path that has few signposts, few definitions. We must know how to trust in ourselves, how to question, and how to learn from our mistakes and detours. We need to know humility, the humility not of subservience but of openness, if we are to survive being assailed by the doubts of others or of self-doubt. It is strength that gives us the energy to persevere in our search for an authentic spiritual vision.

Models of true strength, born of connection, are rare. The models of strength available to us, based upon the capacity to overwhelm and intimidate, are ones many women resist emulating. We may hesitate to develop strength because its adoption appears to imply the sacrifice of our vulnerability and femininity. The models of strength presented to us are invariably ones that express the degeneration of strength. They are models that equate invincibility and invulnerability with strength. Strength, in our culture, is renamed independence. So often it is a negative independence, an independence in which there is a denial and negation of our need for one another, of our connectedness and interdependence. We see the degeneration of strength in aggression, in control, in striving, and in inflexibility.

Women are repeatedly placed in positions of conflict through the mixed messages they receive in their lives. We hear repeatedly of the desirability of adopting the "princess" role in our lives, a role characterized by powerlessness and dependency. We hear repeatedly that our femininity is defined by our vulnerability and sensitivity. The lessons we learn from our culture tell us that success and the achievement of so many goals depends upon our being independent and invulnerable. We feel hindered in our quest for success, both by our conditioning and through our unwillingness to pay the price of success: the sacrifice of our femininity. Just as our capacity for strength can degenerate in our social and professional lives, it can also degenerate easily in our spiritual lives. Spiritual attainment becomes equated with the attainment of invincibility. The capacity to abide unmoved and untouched by the trauma of the world or by inner trauma is regarded as a sign of progress. We are often encouraged to adopt the posture of the spiritual warrior, cutting through, transcending, and overcoming impurities and imperfections. Spiritual development may be presented as an assault, and it is an assault upon our own weaknesses.

The insensitivity that is born of the degeneration of strength is impossible to ignore. Goals become all-important. Intent on achieving our goals of perfection, we are willing to disregard the insensitivity involved in our pursuit of them. Kelsi spoke of the conflicts she created through the confusion she brought to her spiritual life:

> I was the "perfect" candidate for perfection. I brought to my spiritual path immeasurable depths of anxiety and guilt. I was so tired of being a victim. It was a true revelation to be offered a path to being a master. I saw the way to be in control of my life: I just had to become perfect. I wasn't going to let anything distract me from my goal. When

my mother was sick, I praised myself for being unmoved by the pleas from my family to come home. When I went through periods of doubt and anxiety, I congratulated myself for overcoming them. When my menstrual cycles stopped, I even felt I had finally managed to overcome my body. I had so much to transcend it kept me constantly busy, and I enjoyed pitting myself against anything that challenged my pursuit. It was a lonely path and a lonely time, but I even managed to quell those feelings most of the time. It took a long time for me to face the dishonesty of my pursuit. I was trying to become inhuman. I didn't know how to be strong, only how to overcome. The perfection of myself was hard for me to live with, impossible for others.

We see the degeneration of strength in the opinions and standpoints that mar the spiritual life: *I know, I have the answer,* and *I know the truth.* In their longing for security and strength, too many people want to make a personal possession of truth and understanding. We can only be astonished by the number of owners of "the only way" in the spiritual world. Strength degenerates into inflexibility, invincibility, and narrowness because of a lack of insight. The strength that is then portrayed is basically our insecurity and fear dressed and disguised in spiritual terminology.

We need to be cautious and honest, so that our capacity for strength does not degenerate into control, suppression, or the mindless pursuit of goals that will disguise our fear of vulnerability. What we sacrifice in the degeneration of strength is our openness and sensitivity. We become alienated from gentleness and vulnerability. In cultivating a quality of strength that is distorted by fear, we become brutal toward ourselves. We adopt ideals of what a spiritual person is and what we should be experiencing within ourselves. In the very strength of our pursuit of those models and ideals, we become judgmental and dismissive of anything that does not conform to them. Our judgment and prejudice distort every relationship we engage in. We deny all that we perceive as being a weakness within ourselves. In the face of our denial, it becomes increasingly difficult either to accept ourselves totally with love and compassion or to extend that love and compassion to any other relationship. We become hardened in our strength and correspondingly alienated from openness and vulnerability. Too often, we reinforce our own feeling of strength through dwelling upon the weaknesses of others.

We attempt to be strong in order to protect ourselves against threat; at times, we try to be strong in order to protect ourselves against being vulnerable. We need to be strong not so that we can be invulnerable, but so that we can be vulnerable. It takes immense courage to be vulnerable, to be steadfast and strong in our vulnerability. Both strength and vulnerability are essential ingredients in coming to inner wholeness, in discovering freedom without fear.

In Western culture, women are encouraged to cultivate vulnerability and to display that vulnerability in ways that are negative and destructive. We learn to display our vulnerability in negative dependency, in helplessness, and in paralysis. Because those very expressions of vulnerability spell danger for us, we learn to call vulnerability weakness. We have learned to misname vulnerability and devalue this very quality that is so essential to a life of interconnectedness and sensitivity.

Surely we can see that the ability to depend upon other people is crucial to our growth? Surely we can recognize the value in yearning to bond and to connect with others? Any vital, nurturing relationship—whether a parent–child relationship or one between adults—reveals to us the relationship between intimacy and dependency, between connectedness and vulnerability. These qualities are not symptomatic of weakness, but of strength and bonding. Appreciating the wisdom of vulnerability means appreciating the value of relationship and connectedness in our lives. It calls for an inner maturity for us to recognize that you and I live in an undeniable relationship. It is inner maturity and clarity that allow us to recognize that this relationship means that I need you and you need me for our mutual well-being and survival. Our capacity to acknowledge our interconnectedness inspires us to care for one another, to give and receive, and to grow through one another. Our recognition of the relationship that bonds us allows us to utilize its underlying connectedness in order to open and to develop in sensitivity.

Vulnerability holds an important place in our spiritual growth. Characteristics of vulnerability are trust and openness. We need to learn how to discard misplaced trust and naive openness and develop a wise openness and a deep sense of trust based upon inner strength. Such qualities are essential to our discovery of inner wholeness and connectedness with all of life. We need to learn what it means to be open, receptive, and sensitive inwardly. We need to learn what it means to be free from defensiveness and aggressiveness. We need to understand what it means to be free of the burden of opinions and standpoints. We need to know the wisdom integral to the vulnerability of not knowing.

In the vulnerability of not knowing, we abide in a place of openness and learning that will never be discovered if we remain locked within the standpoint of *I know, I am,* or *I have.* To abide in the openness and vulnerability of not knowing, in relationship to ourselves, is important in breaking through the barriers of limited definitions and images we hold of ourselves. Our vulnerability and openness allow us to question with honesty and courage the reality of the images and identities we subscribe to. In that openness, there is the possibility of growth, the possibility of learning, the possibility of connecting with authentic inner wisdom. We see beyond our boundaries to our horizon.

Vulnerability and strength have a further expression in spirituality. They are expressed through both discipline and flexibility, steadfastness and the capacity to yield. These dynamics again are endowed with specific associations: discipline and steadfastness have a masculine association, whereas flexibility and the capacity to yield are valued as feminine.

We may find ourselves shuddering at and resisting the very suggestion of discipline, with all the connotations it may hold for us. We may rightly feel that our lives have been marked by too many commands and decrees governing our behavior, appearance, and life direction. Much of the discipline we have been exposed to in our lives has been imposed upon us by the will of external authorities. Too often, it has been a discipline corrupted by demands for conformity and unquestioning obedience. The inner discipline we employ in our lives is one that is also often corrupted by our own willpower and desire to overcome and transcend. We come to learn that distorted discipline breeds rigidity, tension, and suppression—all experiences from which we want to free ourselves.

We need to be wary that our past associations with a distorted discipline do not lead us to dismiss the value of discipline that is born not of willpower, but of inner clarity and understanding. The object of distorted discipline is conformity. True discipline is radically different in its aim: it is a vehicle that enables us to remain true to all that we value as meaningful in our lives and in ourselves. Discipline is a valuable aid in cutting through the boundaries of our own conditioning.

Jana had a deep commitment to her inner development. It was never easy for her to remain steadfast in her commitment, to continue to take the time to be alone and deepen her understanding. She spoke of the variety of forces that continually seemed to be pulling her away from what she really wanted to do:

> When I used to spend a lot of time in retreat, I would get these endless letters from my family and friends questioning the validity of what I was doing. They pointed out to me that I was getting older and that I had no real career to fall back on when I grew bored with my spiritual interest. They questioned the worth of what I was doing, asking me whether it wasn't something of a fantasy. Their doubts were matched at times by my own inner doubts. At low periods, I, too, questioned the validity of what I was doing. There were times when I, too, felt anxious about the future and not being able to compete in the professional world. Sometimes I doubted my own ability to really discover the mystic within myself. And after a time, I did feel it was appropriate for me to live more in the world. It felt like an organic development and didn't detract at all from my fundamental direction of deepening in understanding. I did marry and have children. I did also continue and sustain my spiritual life. Each time I was pregnant, I was told that now, finally, I would have to settle down. Finding the time to be alone, to be still became more of a challenge with the coming of my babies. Sometimes I felt very attracted to taking a path that seemed easier, to postponing my own development until later. Sometimes I was just tired. It was my commitment to my practice that took me through those times, that led me to see that I didn't have to sacrifice my own development for my children or vice versa. I felt strengthened by the challenge and by my capacity to meet it openheartedly.

True discipline can never be imposed upon us. It is not a taskmaster, but a friend. Superficially, it appears easier to us to indulge ourselves, to avoid the work, or to distract ourselves. Superficially, it appears easier to have our lives directed for us or to flounder than to take responsibility for our own lives and the quality of our inner being. It is not always easy to be alone when we are restless or confused. It is not always pleasant to question ourselves or understand our discontent. It is our inner dedication to what we feel to be true and valuable that sees us through those moments of darkness. That commitment is true discipline; it is an essential ingredient in the emerging of our own sense of wholeness.

It is equally necessary that our discipline be tempered by our capacity to yield and be pliable. It is our flexibility, our capacity to respond to the subtle changes that each moment brings us, that frees us of rigidity and narrowness. Our capacity to yield allows us to open and respond to what is actually happening in each moment in ourselves, rather than what should be happening.

The conditioning of women constantly encourages us to be endlessly yielding and pliable. It is that very conditioning that leads to the degeneration of our pliability. In the degeneration of our pliability, we may become well known for our agreeability. Always willing to compromise, to yield to the needs and expectations of others, we receive much approval for our endless flexibility. Inwardly, we may know that our pliability is no more than an expression of our fear and insecurity, yet we bend repeatedly because we cherish that approval. We fear the consequences of saying no, yet endlessly disempower ourselves through our compliance. We become a reflection of the expectations of others.

Our pliability is in no way diminished by our steadfastness. These are inner dynamics that enhance each other when they exist in balance and rapport. Steadfast in our inner capacity to listen to what we understand to be true and valuable, we are able to open to the input of others and of the moment. Firm in our dedication to all that is true, we are able to question with openness and honesty not only the standpoints and expectations of others, but also our own.

Aspects of our discipline and pliability are our capacities for both agency and receptivity. Inner exploration and the process of nurturing an authentic spiritual vision involves agency: the capacity to change and to transform. We do not come to spirituality with the intention of remaining unchanged. We have aspirations we want to meet: we sense inner and outer changes that need to be made. We look for ways to be effective and empowered to bring about those changes. Our very capacity for agency enables us to call upon our inner resources of energy, attention, and effort to effect transformation.

Yet we must be watchful of mistaking liberation for personal perfection. In pursuing personal perfection, we become habitual in the role of the doer, the modifier. Our mission in that habitual role becomes the conquest of imperfection. We become constantly shadowed by the feeling that we are never quite right, never quite good enough. There is always something more that needs to be changed, needs to be polished, needs to be refined. We come to resemble an interior decorator, constantly dissatisfied with our inner decor. There is validity in nurturing all that contributes to our well-being and understanding. There is validity in freeing ourselves of what is destructive and undermining in ourselves and in our lives. There is, too, deep validity in understanding that the process of substituting one image for another, one personality attribute for another, is endless.

When that understanding dawns upon us, we realize fully that our "problem" does not lie in the images, characteristics, or limitations by which we define ourselves, but that the "problem" is our belief in them. Our only true limitation is believing the untrue to be true, believing the false and conditioned to be our total reality. With that realization comes the understanding that we need to know how to be still, to listen inwardly. We need to listen to the voice of the mystic within, who knows intuitively the boundlessness of our own freedom and our deep interconnectedness with all of life.

In that quality of inner stillness, we know a deep receptivity, a quality of grace. Abiding in grace and receptivity, we are profoundly touched by understanding, by the truth and essence of our being. It is a receptivity that is founded upon inner trust. It is founded upon strength. It is founded upon openness. It is a manifestation of sensitivity and true vulnerability. It is a receptivity in which there is a fulfillment of insight and a fulfillment of our own potential to be conscious, awake, and free women.

Our spiritual path is concerned with wholeness and freedom. It is a path of ending all fragmentation and division within ourselves. We are strong because we are vulnerable. We are pliable and grounded in our dedication to truth. We feel and we articulate our feelings with clarity and effectiveness. We bring forth change and transformation. We abide in grace and receptivity.

Balance and rapport among all the dynamics that exist within ourselves enhances and contributes to our own sense of inner wholeness and freedom. We are free to call upon our inner dynamics as vehicles for awakening when we acknowledge their relatedness and the need for their balance. The awakened woman emerges from the chrysalis of her own inner resources. She is established in freedom, and she manifests her freedom in the celebration of her interconnectedness with all of life.

# Chapter 7
## *Closing*

O<small>N EITHER SIDE</small> of the turning points in our lives, there are endings and new beginnings. Our new beginnings are made possible by the endings we bring about. New and fresh ways of being and relating, and a new sense of who we are, are born of leaving behind us all that undermines our dignity, spirit, and integrity. Inevitably, the unfoldment of inner wisdom instigates an organic process of opening new horizons and discoveries for us. It is a process from which there is no turning back. Once we discover the joy of being awake, it is no longer possible for us to reconcile ourselves to a life of limitation or unconsciousness. We must listen to the voice of the mystic within, which speaks to us of our potential to be whole, to be free, and to be at one with the heart of life.

It will not always be easy for us to heed the mystic within ourselves. We feel anxiety in leaving behind the familiarity and comfort of the past. We feel apprehensive when the future offers us no guarantees. We will have moments when we are assailed by doubts, our own and the doubts of others. There will be times when we feel psychologically, emotionally, and spiritually uncertain of our path to freedom and our capacity to undertake it. We will also learn how to open our hearts to those moments, with acceptance and gentleness. In learning how to do this, we will not be overwhelmed by our anxieties or doubts. Our vision of our own potential and fulfillment will not be obscured.

Without endings, there can be no beginnings. The endings we bring about on our spiritual journey do not imply rejection, dismissal, or condemnation. Making new beginnings does not demand that we forsake our relationships, our lifestyles, or the traditions that have nourished us. Making new beginnings does not necessarily imply the adoption of new belief systems, new hierarchies, or new identities. Changing our values, our life directions, or our models does not confirm new beginnings for us. New beginnings are rooted in inner transformation and wisdom. New beginnings are rooted in inner trust and understanding, not in bitterness and resentment.

The trust and understanding that emerge from within us make themselves visible in the relationship we form with the world around us and with ourselves. It is a relationship that honors and cherishes the spirit and integrity of all life. It is an inner relationship that honors wholeness and freedom above all else. It is a relationship of love and of compassion. Living within this relationship, we are called upon to bring to an end anything— structures, values, stereotypes, or models—that denies the wholeness and connectedness we perceive and honor.

Honoring this relationship, we will seek to bring an end to structures and institutions that hold in contempt the spirit and integrity of any life. We will seek to end any institution that is founded upon greed, a belief in separation, or distorted power. Trusting in our effectiveness and our connectedness with all of life, we will no longer accept social, political, or spiritual values or belief systems that do not honor the fundamental interconnectedness of all life.

Our capacity to transform the world we live in is rooted in our capacity to bring to an end within ourselves the limitations and restrictions that undermine our own freedom and integrity. We are empowered to make new beginnings in our lives by leaving behind us the false identities and the negative belief systems concerning who we are that cripple our vision of inner freedom and wholeness. We are able to discard the models and images of who we should be through our dedication to discovering the truth of who we are. This fundamental understanding is what empowers us to discard the false. It is not an understanding that can be gifted to us by anyone or anything else, nor can it ever be taken from us. It is an understanding that is born of our own courage and inquiry. It is an understanding that is liberating.

The endings we bring about, inwardly and outwardly, are not manifestations of conclusions we have reached about ourselves or the world. Conclusions imply reaching fixed standpoints, assuming a rigid and static way of seeing. Surely one lesson we have learned in the development of our own understanding is the liability of holding on to any rigid, frozen way of seeing. What we need to leave behind in developing a sensitive and learning relationship to life and ourselves are all the conclusions that have hindered us in our lives. Conclusions in the form of stereotypes, models, and belief systems have served to make us invisible as awake, conscious women. Conclusions are too often defenses, which are only barriers to learning. Our endings are not conclusions, but openings that are new beginnings.

Through our openness and understanding, we make ourselves visible as awake and conscious women with specific contributions to offer. We offer our vision, our inner vision, our vision of life. We offer and manifest a way of seeing and a way of being that are rooted in interconnectedness, wisdom, and balance. We offer a vision that is healing and liberating. We manifest a way of being that respects and honors the life, spirit, and freedom of all life. It is our spiritual heritage: it is the essence of our being.

Connected with our spiritual heritage and the essence of our being, we speak with a voice that is echoed by countless other women. We are empowered and strengthened by that connection. We embark upon our new beginnings with joy, love, and celebration. We embark upon our new beginnings as women who are awake.

# *Notes*

CHAPTER 2: FAIRY TALES

1. Faith Wilding, "Waiting," in Judy Chicago, *Through the Flower: My Struggles as a Woman Artist*, Anchor Press/Doubleday, New York, 1975.
2. Carolyn Heilbrun, *Reinventing Womanhood*, W. W. Norton & Co., New York, 1979, p. 146.
3. Karen Rowe, "Feminism and Fairy Tales," cited in Heilbrun, *Reinventing Womanhood*, p. 146.
4. Introduction to Mary E. Giles (ed.), *The Feminist Mystic*, Crossroad Publishing Co., New York, 1982.
5. Adrienne Rich, *Lies, Secrets, Silence*, Virago, London, 1980.
6. Emily Dickinson, "Me from Myself—to banish," in Thomas H. Johnson, ed., *The Complete Poems of Emily Dickinson*, Little, Brown, Boston, 1960, pp. 318–19.

CHAPTER 3: THE UNNATURAL DIVORCE

1. Daniel D. Williams, *Spirit and Forms of Love*, Harper & Row, New York, 1968, p. 220.
2. Tertullian, *De cultu feminarum*, cited in Mary E. Giles (ed.), *The Feminist Mystic*, Crossroad Publishing Co., New York, 1982, p. 122.
3. Jules Toner, S.J., *What Is Love?* Corpus, Washington, D.C., 1968, p. 41ff.
4. Anne Bancroft, *Women in Buddhism*, an unpublished paper.
5. *Meister Eckhart: A Modern Translation*, trs. Raymond B. Blakney, Harper & Row, New York, 1941, p. 102.

CHAPTER 5: POWER

1. George Wald, "The Human Enterprise," in Noel Hinrichs (ed.), *Population, Environment and People*, McGraw-Hill, New York, 1971, p. 222.

2. Barbara Ehrenreich and Deirdre English, *Witches, Midwives and Nurses,* The Feminist Press, Old Westbury, N.Y., 1973, pp. 7–8.

3. Heinrich Kramer and James Sprenger, *Malletur Maleficarum,* Dover Publications, New York, 1971, p. 66.

4. "Charge of the Star Goddess," from the Western Pagan Traditional, quoted by Hallie Iglehart in "Expanding Personal Power through Meditation," in Charlene Spretnak (ed.), *The Politics of Women's Spirituality,* Anchor Press/Doubleday, New York, 1982, p. 303.

5. Meinrad Craighead, "Immanent Mother," in Mary E. Giles (ed.), *The Feminist Mystic,* Crossroad Publishing Co., New York, 1982, p. 71.

# *Appreciations*

G RATEFUL ACKNOWLEDGMENT is made to the following for permission to reprint previously published material:

# About the Author

In the early 1970s, Christina Feldman spent several years in Asia, studying and training in the Buddhist meditation tradition. She has led insight mediation retreats in the West since 1974. A cofounder of Gaia House, in Devon, England, she is a regular teacher at the Insight Meditation Society in Barre, Massachusetts, and at Spirit Rock in Woodacre, California. In addition, she leads retreats in Europe.

She is the coauthor (with Jack Kornfield) of *Soul Food*, and the author of *Quest of the Warrior Woman, Ways of Meditation*, and *Buddhist Path to Simplicity*, as well as *Silence* and *Woman Awake*. She lives in Totnes, Devon, England.

For more information, visit www.gaiahouse.co.uk.

# Index